# American Folktales, I

*A Structured Reader*

# American Folktales, I

*A Structured Reader*

**Vinal O. Binner**

*Thomas Y. Crowell*
*HARPER & ROW, PUBLISHERS*
*New York   Hagerstown   San Francisco   London*

AMERICAN FOLKTALES/I: A Structured Reader

Library of Congress Catalog Card Number: 66-14932
ISBN 0-690-06704-6

## ACKNOWLEDGMENTS

For permission to adapt copyrighted stories for this reader, acknowledgment is extended to the following:

B. A. Botkin, "Salting the Pudding," from *A Treasury of American Folklore,* Crown Publishers, Inc. By permission of B. A. Botkin.

Richard Chase, "The Cure" and "That's Once," from *American Folk Tales and Songs.* Copyright © 1956 by Richard Chase, by permission of The New American Library, New York.

Zora Neale Hurston, "High Walker and Bloody Bones," "The Son Who Went to College," and "The Talking Mule," from *Mules and Men,* J. B. Lippincott Co. Copyright 1920 by Zora Neale Hurston. By permission of Joel Hurston and John C. Hurston.

M. Jagendorf, "Hans the Butter Man" reprinted by permission of the publisher, The Vanguard Press, from *Upstate, Downstate: Folk Stories of the Middle Atlantic States,* by M. Jagendorf. Copyright 1949, by M. Jagendorf.

*Journal of American Folklore,* "Gally Mander" and "Jack-O-My Lantern: A Maryland Version," from *Folklore of Maryland,* by Annie Weston Whitney and Caroline Canfield Bullock. By permission of the American Folklore Society, Inc.

# Preface

## FOR THE TEACHER

Folktales can be used with groups of diverse ages and cultural backgrounds. They have a wide appeal, as they deal with matters of universal interest: families, animals, human foibles, the supernatural, and death. These stories, retold for the student of English, present a view of American folk roots not available before now to a student at this level of language mastery.

The stories provide fertile material for conversation, retelling, comparisons, and contrasts; and the traditional form of the folktale, with its extensive use of dialogue, reinforces the teaching of natural patterns useful for both conversation and informal writing.

As the subtitle of this book, *A Structured Reader,* suggests, the retelling of these stories has been carried out with a specific purpose. In each unit, selected structures are presented several times in the context of the story. In the study section following the story, the sentences are identified as examples of particular structures and the use of the structures is explained. Pattern sentences for visual and oral reinforcement are followed by exercises eliciting, wherever possible, the structural patterns in the response. It is expected that teachers and students both will find this a meaningful, effective approach to some of the basic grammatical structures of English.

It is assumed that the student knows the basic vocabulary and grammar taught in a first course in English. Vocabulary is carefully controlled throughout the text and not more than 300 new root words are added to the approximately 1,000 basic words. Emphasis is on commonly used derivatives and on the different forms of a word rather than on unrelated words. All words used in the text are listed in the Vocabulary section at the back of the

vii

book, and those that might require special study are listed after the reading selection in each unit. I have found that students are greatly helped by having the various forms of words spelled out. The Vocabulary includes the gerund and participles of all verbs, the plural form of nouns, and the comparative and superlative forms of adjectives and adverbs. It also includes common phrases, listings showing the use of mass nouns, and the most common verb-preposition phrases (e.g., **to wake up, to fall down**). Where a certain preposition is commonly used with a given transitive verb, this is shown as a complete phrase, such as **to talk about** (**something**). The student has at hand continual reinforcement in correctly distinguishing transitive verbs and in using them with most common prepositions and word order. This section can serve as a valuable reference tool, facilitating independent use of new and previously studied words.

The presentation of individual words is also more organized than is usual in a reader. The vocabulary at the end of each story includes lists of "Related Words" (those having a common root with the vocabulary word) and selected "Opposites." These sections enable the student to enrich his vocabulary with clusters of meaningfully related words, and promote variety in classroom discussions and exercises. Whether or not these words are presented fully, it is expected that they will prove useful during study of the unit in which they appear.

Of the twenty questions asked in each Conversation section, the first ten test the student's comprehension of the subject matter in the story, and the second ten ask him to relate the story and new vocabulary to his own experience or frame of reference.

The Glossary of Grammatical Terms, Table of Punctuation Marks, Guide to Pronunciation, and comprehensive Vocabulary may be of continuing use not only throughout the course of study but after its completion.

## FOR THE STUDENT

This book is for you. It has been designed to help you understand easily and learn quickly.

### Punctuation marks

When you write English, you will want to understand the use of punctuation marks. The names of the marks you will need to learn to use are on page 139. You should practice using these marks when you write dictation exercises.

### Pronunciation

The guide on page 140 gives you symbols for all English sounds. If you learn to read these symbols you can see how to pronounce words when you have no teacher to help you.

### Grammatical terms

Definitions of grammatical terms are on pages 141 to 148. If you don't understand or remember a grammatical term, look for it on these pages.

### Vocabulary

All new vocabulary words are in a list at the end of each story. There you will also find lists of "Opposites" and "Related Words," to help you in your conversation and writing. All words used in the book are listed at the end of the book on pages 149 to 173. There you can find the plural form of each noun, the different forms of adjectives and adverbs, and the main forms of each verb. If a word is new in this book, you will find beside it in the Vocabulary the number of the unit where it was first used.

—*V.O.B.*

# Contents

**APPENDIXES**

# Unit 1

# Two Davy Crockett Stories

*Davy Crockett is a popular American folk hero. He was a real person, but today we remember him for the funny stories about him instead of for the exciting things he did. He liked to tell stories about himself. For a long time he was a congressman. In Congress, too, he liked to tell funny stories about himself before he began to talk about serious things. These stories are like many others he told.*

   ✿   ✿   ✿

Two or three times a year I see the badman of the Ohio River, the boatman Mike Fink. We are friendly enemies. Once Mike sent me a letter. In the letter he invited me to a shooting match. He can shoot well, but I can shoot better. However, I lost this match.

When I had time, I visited Mike Fink at his home. I got my gun ready for shooting.

"You shoot first," said Mike.

"All right," I said, and I shot at a cat a hundred and fifty yards away. The shot took the hair from its head, but the cat didn't move. It didn't know its hair was gone.

"Not bad," said Mike.

Then the cat began to wash its head. When it found its hair was gone, it turned its back and ran. That was a lucky cat, because now Mike Fink was looking for something to shoot at.

When his gun was ready to shoot, he shot at a chicken. That chicken was at the end of the earth. When Mike's gun was empty, the chicken had only one feather on its back.

"That's good shooting," I said politely, and then I shot off the *last* feather. That made me very happy, but Mike didn't say, "Very good!" this time. Instead he looked for another place to shoot. The chicken was hiding now, but Mike saw his wife instead. She went to the river three times a day to get water. Mike saw her walking up from the river with a pitcher of water in her hands. In her hair was a small comb, and he shot away half of it.

"Be still," Mike called to her. "Davy Crockett wants to shoot next." Mrs. Fink stood very still.

"Try to shoot away the other half of the comb," said Mike.

"No, no, Mike," I said. "I'm too polite to shoot at a woman. You win the match, Mike."

❋   ❋   ❋

One time I was out with my gun. I was at a place called Great Gap when I saw a raccoon up in a tree. When I pointed my gun at him, he put up one paw and asked, "Is your name Crockett?"

"That's right," I said. "My name is Davy Crockett."

"Then you don't have to shoot," said the raccoon, "because I'm coming down. I know I can't hide from you, even if I run to the ends of the earth." He walked down the tree to me and stood still.

I didn't move, and he said finally, "Here I am. Why don't you shoot me?"

I couldn't shoot that raccoon. I patted him on the head and said, "I'll shoot myself before I shoot a hair off your head. I never heard a better compliment."

"I'm glad you think that," said the raccoon. "Now I'll go away. I believe you, but I don't want to be here when you change your mind."

## Vocabulary

| | | | |
|---|---|---|---|
| all right | feather | instead | related |
| away | finally | like | to remember |
| to change | folk | to lose | river |
| chicken | following | match | to send |
| comb | friendly | mind | to shoot |
| to complete | gun | opposite | shooting match |
| compliment | hair | to pat | shot |
| Congress | happy | paw | someone |
| to connect | head | pitcher | still |
| empty | hero | polite | to turn |
| enemy | to hide | raccoon | |

## Idioms

at the end of the earth,
   to the ends of the earth
to change one's mind
to get (something) ready
to go away
to be gone
to have time
how often
instead of (something)
to be like (something)

to look for (something)
to point (something) at
   (something)
to put (something) up
to shoot (something)
to shoot (something) away, to
   shoot (something) off
this time
to turn one's back

## Related Words

comb (noun)
to comb (verb)

Congress (noun)
congressman (noun)

empty (adj.)
to empty (verb)
emptiness (noun)

finally (adv.)
final (adj.)

following (adj.)
following (noun)
to follow (verb)

happy (adj.)
happily (adv.)
happiness (noun)

polite (adj.)
politely (adv.)
politeness (noun)

to shoot (verb)
shooting (adj.)
shot (noun)

still (adj.)
stillness (noun)

## Opposites

empty—full
enemy—friend
happy—sad
to lose—to find
polite—rude, impolite
to remember—to forget
to send—to receive, to get
still—noisy

## Structure

### I. ADVERBIAL PHRASES OF TIME

*From your reading:*

**Two or three times a year** I see my friend Mike Fink.
She went to the river **three times a day** to get water.

*An adverbial phrase of time may answer the question, How often?*

### A. Read these sentences:

**How often** does he come here?
He comes here **once a day.**
He comes here **once a week.**

He comes here **once a month.**
He comes here **once a year.**

**How often** did you see your brother?
I saw him **once a month.**
I saw him **twice a day.**
I saw him **three times a week.**
I saw him **ten times a year.**

B. *Answer these questions, using the phrase in parentheses in your answer:*

1. How often do you go to class? (twice a day)
2. How often does John take a trip? (about once a year)
3. How often do they eat chicken? (three times a month)
4. How often do we study English? (once a day)
5. How often does she go to the dentist? (two or three times a year)
6. How often did you speak English last year? (four or five times a day)
7. How often did you visit your friend? (once or twice a week)
8. How often did he see you? (once a week)
9. How often did Mike drink a glass of water? (about three times a day)
10. How often did they hide from Mike Fink? (only once)

## II. ADVERBIAL CLAUSES WITH <u>WHEN</u>

*From your reading:*

**When I had time,** I visited Mike Fink.
I was at a place called Great Gap **when I saw a raccoon up in a tree.**

A. *Read these sentences. Notice that the adverbial clause may be either at the beginning or the end of the sentence:*

When he visits her, she cooks chicken.
She cooks chicken when he visits her.

We drink water when we are thirsty.
When we are thirsty, we drink water.

**Structure** (continued)

**B. Connect the following sentences, using _when_ and a comma:**

*Example: We go to school. We learn English.*
*       When we go to school, we learn English.*

1. The pitcher is empty. She fills it with water.
2. The apples are green. We don't eat them.
3. We go to school. My mother washes the dishes.
4. I don't understand the lesson. I have to study.
5. The weather is good. He likes to walk by the river.
6. She was happy. She sang a song.
7. He is thirsty. He drinks water.
8. The boys were hungry. They ate chicken.
9. The cat saw Davy Crockett. It hid in the grass.
10. He saw a raccoon in a tree. He was happy.

**C. Read and complete the following sentences:**

*Example: When the teacher comes, we _____.*
*       When the teacher comes, we open our books.*

1. When the door is open, I _____.
2. We _____ when we come to school.
3. When I write on the blackboard, I _____.
4. When the class ends, the students _____.
5. I _____ when I go home.
6. When I see a cat, I _____.
7. When my glass is empty, I _____.
8. My father _____ when I come to school.
9. The boys _____ when their mother calls them.
10. I _____ when I don't understand a new word.

# Conversation

*Answer the following questions, using complete sentences:*

1. For what do many people remember Davy Crockett?
2. Where did he like to tell stories about himself?

3. How often did Davy Crockett see Mike Fink?
4. Why did Mike invite Davy to visit him?
5. How far away was the cat when Davy shot at it?
6. Why did the cat run and hide?
7. What was in Mrs. Fink's hands?
8. What did Mrs. Fink have in her hair?
9. Where was the raccoon?
10. Why did the raccoon go away?
11. Is there a comb on the teacher's table?
12. Did the teacher point to the blackboard?
13. Did you ever send a letter to a friend?
14. Is the classroom empty now?
15. Do you know a folk story?
16. Who are some other popular heroes?
17. Is this the final day of school?
18. Did you drink a glass of water at lunchtime?
19. Did you ever see a football match?
20. Did you ever see a raccoon?

## Write or Tell

*A Friend Visits Our Home*

*A Folk Hero*

## Dictation

*Listen to, repeat, and then write each of the following sentences:*

Davy Crockett seldom lost a shooting match. He could shoot very well, but when he visited his friendly enemy, Mike Fink, he didn't want to shoot at a woman's comb. He was too polite. Mike Fink was noisy and impolite, but he could shoot well, and his wife could stand very still.

## Pronunciation

| / æ / | / b / | / p / |
|-------|-------|-------|
| happy | boy | pitcher |
| raccoon | back | pat |
| sat | before | happy |
| pat | because | put |

/ æ /    "I am happy and glad," said Pat, and sat down.

/ p /    The happy child played with the pitcher.

/ b /    The boy turned his back because he wanted to see the blackboard.

/ b, p /  The boy took the pitcher and put it by the door.

# Unit 2

# The Talking Mule

Once upon a time there was a man who owned a mule and a dog. The mule's name was Bill. The dog had no name at all.

Early every morning the man went to his field to get his mule. He always said, "Come here, Bill," and the mule came.

One morning the man slept late. When he got out of bed, he drank a cup of coffee. Then his eyes began to open, and he thought about his mule. He wanted to eat breakfast, and his wife did, too, so he called his son and said, "Go to the field for me, Son, and get the mule."

---

Adapted from Zora Neale Hurston, "The Talking Mule."

The boy liked to get the mule. He took a rope for the animal and ran to the field.

"Come here, Bill," he said.

The mule didn't move. He stood and looked at the boy.

The boy said, "Don't stand there and look at me. Pa wants you this morning. Come here and put your head through this rope."

But the mule only looked at the boy and said, "Every morning someone says, 'Come here, Bill.' I want to sleep in the morning, but someone always says, 'Come here, Bill.'"

The boy's eyes opened wide, and he dropped the rope. He was a boy who could run fast, and now he did. He ran back to the house and said to his father, "That mule is talking!"

"Now, Son, don't tell me a lie. Go get the mule."

"I'm telling the truth, Pa. That mule is talking. You have to get him yourself. I can't. I'm afraid."

The man shook his head. He turned to his wife and said, "Listen to the boy. I don't think he is telling the truth."

"I don't either," said his wife.

Then the man got up from the table and went to the field. His dog went, too. The mule was eating grass.

"Come here, Bill."

The old mule slowly lifted his head. He looked the man in the eye and said, "Every morning somebody says, 'Come here, Bill.' Go home now and let me eat my breakfast."

When he heard the mule talk, the man began to run, and his dog did, too. The man ran home. His wife was at the door.

"The boy did tell the truth," said the man. "That mule does talk. I never heard a mule talk before."

The little dog was sitting by the man's feet. He looked up and said, "I never heard a mule talk, either."

Then the man began to run from his dog. He ran into the woods, but the little dog ran with him. That man almost died.

Finally he had to stop by a tree to rest. He said, "I'm so tired, I can't run any more."

The little dog sat down at the man's feet. He breathed hard and said, "I'm tired, too."

The man is still running.

## Vocabulary

| | | | |
|---|---|---|---|
| affirmative | either | negative | someone |
| afraid | eye | rope | to stand |
| animal | foot, feet | to shake | to stop |
| to breathe | lie | simple | substitute |
| to die | to lift | slowly | truth |
| to drop | mule | somebody | woods |

## Idioms

to be afraid

to get up

to look (someone) in the eye

once upon a time

to tell a lie

to tell the truth

to be tired

## Related Words

to breathe (verb)
breath (noun)

to die (verb)
dead (adj.)
death (noun)

lie (noun)
to lie (verb)

quickly (adv.)
quick (adj.)

slowly (adv.)
slow (adj.)

truth (noun)
true (adj.)
truthful (adj.)

to stop (verb)
stop (noun)

# Opposites

afraid—unafraid
to get up—to sit down
a lie—the truth
slowly—quickly
to stop—to start, to begin

# Structure

## I. THE SUBSTITUTE VERB <u>DO</u>

*From your reading:*

He wanted to eat breakfast, and his wife **did,** too.
The man began to run, and his dog **did,** too.

A. *Instead of repeating a simple verb (and its complements) in a sentence or in two related sentences, we often use a form of the auxiliary <u>do</u> alone.*

She likes cookies, and her little brother does, too. (*Instead of,* She likes cookies, and her little brother likes cookies.)

They don't want to see him, and I don't, either. (*Instead of,* They don't want to see him and I don't want to see him.)

B. *Use <u>do</u>, <u>does</u>, or <u>did</u> in each of these sentences:*

*Example:* Who studied the lesson? She _____.
          Who studied the lesson? She did.

1. He came at eight o'clock, and I _____, too.
2. They wrote the exercise. _____ you?
3. He doesn't want to sing. _____ you?
4. He doesn't say much, but his sister _____.
5. Our class speaks English. The other class _____, too.
6. Who opens the window every morning? The teacher

_____.

7. He wants a car. His brother _____, too.
8. My mother cooks breakfast. _____ your mother?
9. He wanted to learn English, and his sister _____, too.
10. This year she studies that book. Last year her brother _____.

## II. EITHER AND TOO

*From your reading:*

He went to the field. His dog went, too.
The man began to run, and the dog did, too.

"I don't believe him," said the man.
"I don't, either," said his wife.

"I never heard a mule talk before."
"I never heard a mule talk, either."

*Too is used in affirmative sentences, and either in negative sentences.*

### A. *Read the sentences:*

The mule spoke. The dog spoke.
The mule spoke, and the dog did, too.

The boy went to the field. The man went to the field.
The boy went to the field, and the man did, too.

I got up early. My father got up early.
I got up early, and my father did, too.

The boy didn't sing. The mule didn't sing.
The boy didn't sing, and the mule didn't, either.

I wasn't tired. He wasn't tired.
I wasn't tired, and he wasn't, either.

My son doesn't run. My son doesn't speak.
My son doesn't run, and he doesn't speak, either.

### B. *Connect the following sentences with and, using too or either:*

*Example: He is unafraid. His mother is unafraid.*
*He is unafraid, and his mother is, too.*

**Structure (continued)**

1. I'm not big. My brother isn't big.
2. He told the truth. His father told the truth.
3. The mule could talk. The dog could talk.
4. The farmer doesn't lie. His son doesn't lie.
5. I don't have a mule. My friend doesn't have a mule.
6. He stopped to rest by a tree. The dog stopped to rest by a tree.
7. He didn't believe the boy. She didn't believe the boy.
8. The mule wasn't afraid. The mother wasn't afraid.
9. The farmer ran through the field. The dog ran through the field.
10. The boy didn't move. The mule didn't move.

## III. THE RELATIVE PRONOUN <u>WHO</u>

*From your reading:*

Once there was a man who owned a mule and a dog.
He was a boy who could run fast.
The man who owned the mule slept late.

**A. Read the following questions and answer them, using the phrase in parentheses:**

*Example: Who isn't here? (the boy who knows English)*
*The boy who knows English isn't here.*

1. Who was by the tree? (the man who owned the house)
2. Who wrote the exercise? (the student who had the pencil)
3. Who is in the classroom? (the teacher who teaches English)
4. Who wants water? (a man who is thirsty)
5. Who was late to class? (the girl who slept late)
6. Who plays football? (the boy who speaks slowly)
7. Who was afraid? (the man who owned the mule)
8. Who closed the door? (the person who came in last)

9. Who dropped his book? (the student who is by the door)
10. Who got the mule? (the boy who had the rope)

**B. Connect the following sentences, using the relative pronoun _who_:**

Example: *Bill is a boy. He goes to school.*
*Bill is a boy who goes to school.*

1. A farmer is a man. He lives on a farm.
2. John is a boy. He has brown eyes.
3. Did you see the girl? She stood in the field.
4. There is the man. He shook my hand.
5. Mr. Smith was an old man. He died yesterday.
6. Anna is the girl. She sits beside the window.
7. Mr. Smith was a man. He usually told the truth.
8. Look at the man. He is lifting the table.
9. Where is the girl? She saw the dog.
10. Do you know the teacher? He teaches English.
11. This is the girl. She ran a long way.
12. John is the oldest boy. He studies here.
13. The man spoke to the girl. She was his daughter.
14. The woman has a dog. He likes to run.
15. I have a friend. He can speak three languages.

## Conversation

*Answer the following questions, using complete sentences:*

1. What was the mule's name?
2. Where did the mule stay at night?
3. Was the boy afraid? Why?
4. What did the man do when he got out of bed?
5. Did the boy tell the truth?
6. What was the mule doing when the man went to the field?
7. Did the mule like to work?

**Conversation** (continued)

8. Who was at the door of the house?
9. Do you know the dog's name?
10. Where did the man stop to rest?
11. Are you afraid of a talking mule?
12. Are there woods near the school?
13. Do you like to sleep late in the morning?
14. Who is sitting beside you?
15. When do you stop studying at night?
16. Is it true that chalk is black?
17. Did you drop your pencil?
18. Is it hard to read when you are sleepy?
19. How many feet does a person have? How many heads? How many eyes?
20. Do you know someone who likes animals?

## Write or Tell

*An Interesting Animal*

*I Am Afraid of . . .*

## Dictation

*Listen to the dictation read by your teacher. Repeat each sentence and then write it:*

A farmer who owned a dog slept late. His son went to the field to get the mule. The mule said, "Let me sleep in the morning." The boy was afraid, and his father was, too. The father ran through the woods with his dog. His wife didn't run, and his son didn't either. "I'm so tired, I don't know what to do," the man said.

# Pronunciation

| / ɑ / | / d / | / t / |
|-------|-------|-------|
| got | dog | talk |
| hard | drank | tired |
| want | head | truth |
| Pa | bed | tell |

/ ɑ /  Pa wanted the hard chair.

/ d /  The dog's head is near the bed.

/ t /  The tired mule told the truth.

/ d, t /  The tired dog drank tea.

# Unit 3

# The Stingy Old Woman

Once there was a stingy old woman. She didn't spend any money.
She ate only dry bread and drank only water. But she had a bag
with lots of gold and silver in it. She put the bag in her chimney.

The old woman's servant girl knew there was a bag of money,
and she looked for it. One evening the servant girl cooked supper.
After supper the old woman wanted to visit a friend. She said
to the girl, "Don't look up the chimney."

Then the old woman left the house, and the girl was by herself.

Adapted from *Journal of American Folklore,* "Gally Mander."

She looked up the chimney. There she saw the bag of money. She opened the bag, saw lots of silver and gold, took it, and ran away.

On the road the girl talked to herself about what she would buy with the money. "I'll get myself a new dress," she said.

After a time the girl passed a cow on the road. The old cow said. "Oh, come, pretty girl, and milk me."

"I don't have time to milk you, old cow," the girl said. "I'm running away."

After a time she met an old horse. "Oh, come, pretty girl, and wash my dirty back," said the horse.

"I don't have time to wash your dirty old back," the girl said. "Wash it yourself."

After a time she passed an apple tree with lots of apples on it. "Oh, come, pretty girl, and pick some of my apples," said the tree. "I'm tired of holding them."

"I don't have time to pick your old apples," said the girl. And she ran on.

The old woman came home and saw the girl was gone. She looked up the chimney and saw her money was gone. Then she ran along the road and yelled, "My gold and silver are gone!"

Soon she met the cow. "Old cow, did you see a girl with a bag of money?"

"Yes, I did, old woman. Run and catch her," said the cow.

After a time she met the old horse. "Old horse, did you see a girl with a bag of money?"

"Yes, old woman. Run and catch her."

The old woman came to the apple tree. "Apple tree, did you see a girl with a bag of money?"

"Yes, old woman, she went along this road."

The old woman ran along the road and caught the girl. She beat her and took the bag of money. Then she went home.

The old woman lived by herself a long time. Then she got another servant girl. The old woman liked the new girl very much. One evening she said, "I'm going to visit a friend. Don't look up the chimney."

Now the girl wanted to look up the chimney, and she did. She saw the bag of money and took it. Then the bad servant girl ran away from the house and along the road. She passed the old cow.

"Pretty girl, come and milk me," said the cow.

"Yes, I'll milk you, old cow," the girl said, and she milked the cow.

Soon she came to the old horse. "Pretty girl, please wash my dirty back," said the horse.

"Yes, I'll wash it," she said, and she washed it and washed it. Then she saw that she was dirty, so she washed herself, too.

After a time she came to the apple tree. "Pretty girl, will you pick some of my apples?"

"Yes, I'll pick them," she said, and she picked and picked. Then the apple tree said, "I didn't think you would help me. Thank you. Now get up into my branches. The old woman is coming." The girl lifted herself into the tree.

When the old woman went home, she looked up the chimney. She saw her bag of money was gone, so she ran outdoors and along the road.

"Old cow, did you see a girl with my money?"

"Yes. She came by a long time ago."

The old woman met the horse. "Old horse, did you see a girl with a bag of money?"

"Yes, but she came by a long time ago."

Then the stingy old woman came to the apple tree. "Apple tree, did you see the girl with my bag of money?"

"I forget," said the apple tree.

"What shall I do? What shall I do?" asked the old woman.

The apple tree said, "Go home and eat dry bread the rest of your life."

And the stingy old woman had to do it. She lived alone and did all the work herself.

The servant girl had to stay in the apple tree. She couldn't climb down with the bag of money, and she didn't want to climb down without it. Some people say she is there today.

## Vocabulary

| | | | |
|---|---|---|---|
| alone | to climb | horse | statement |
| along | cow | to milk | stingy |
| away | dirty | oneself | supper |
| bag | down | to pass | without |
| to beat | dry | to pick | to yell |
| branch | emphasis | rest | |
| to catch | gold | servant | |
| chimney | to hold | silver | |

## Idioms

after a time

to live alone

by oneself

the rest of (something)

to run away

to be tired of (something)

## Related Words

alone (adv.)
loneliness (noun)
lonely (adj.)

to climb (verb)
climber (noun)

dirty (adj.)
dirt (noun)

dry (adj.)
to dry (verb)

gold (noun)
gold (adj.)
golden (adj.)

to milk (verb)
milk (noun)

servant (noun)
to serve (verb)

silver (noun)
silver (adj.)

without (prep.)
with (prep.)

## Opposites

dirty—clean
down—up
dry—wet
stingy—generous
without—with

# Structure

## I. NOUN CLAUSES AS OBJECTS OF <u>THINK</u>, <u>KNOW</u>, <u>SAY</u>, <u>SEE</u>; USE OF <u>THAT</u>

*From your reading:*

"I didn't **think you would help** me."
The girl **knew there was** a bag of money.
Some people **say she is** there today.
The old woman **saw the girl was** gone.

**A.** *Between these verbs and their noun clause objects,* <u>*that*</u> *is sometimes used and sometimes not used.*

She ate only dry bread.
I **know** (**that**) she ate only dry bread.

The old woman came home.
He **thinks** (**that**) the old woman came home.

She was stingy.
They **said** (**that**) she was stingy.

REVIEW NOTE: *Some other words used sometimes with* <u>*that*</u> *and sometimes without are* <u>*agree*</u>, <u>*feel*</u>, <u>*hear*</u>, *and* <u>*believe*</u>.

I **agree** (**that**) the old woman was stingy.
**Do** you **believe** (**that**) the girl is in the tree now?

**B.** *In this exercise, each sentence is followed by a clause in parentheses. Make one sentence, using the sentence and the clause. Make the sentence first using* <u>*that*</u> *and then make it again without using* <u>*that*</u>.

*Example: We studied last night. (The teacher knows)*
        *The teacher knows that we studied last night.*
        *The teacher knows we studied last night.*

1. She ran along the road. (I think)
2. The bag was full of gold. (He saw)
3. The old woman caught the first servant girl. (You know)
4. You want to look up the chimney. (I think)

5. The blackboard is dirty. (We see)
6. She likes to eat dry bread. (She says)
7. They milked the cow. (They said)
8. We aren't stingy. (Other people say)
9. The girl was in the branches. (The old woman didn't know)
10. The girl climbed up the tree. (She didn't think)
11. We picked all the apples. (He didn't know)
12. The horse was old. (We didn't see)
13. The floor is dry. (We can see)
14. They yelled at the football game. (The boys said)
15. There was a football game. (We didn't know)

## II. REFLEXIVE PRONOUNS

**A.**

|          | *Singular* | *Plural* |
|----------|-----------|----------|
| 1st person | myself | ourselves |
| 2nd person | yourself | yourselves |
| 3rd person | himself | themselves |
|          | herself |  |
|          | itself |  |

**B.** *Reflexive pronouns are used as indirect objects.*

**She** washed **herself.**
The **girl** lifted **herself** into the tree.
"**I'll** get **myself** a new dress."

**C.** *Reflexive pronouns are used as objects of prepositions.*

The **girl** talked **to herself.**
**He** bought candy **for himself.**

**D.** *The phrase by oneself means alone.*

The girl was **by herself.**
The old woman lived **by herself.**

**E.** *Reflexive pronouns are also used for emphasis.*

Wash it **yourself.**
She did all the work **herself.**

Structure (continued)

**F. Read these sentences and use the reflexive pronoun for the indicated noun or pronoun:**

*Example: He got the book for _____.*
*He got the book for himself.*

1. Do **you** often read to _____?
2. She wanted to sit down, so **she** got _____ a chair.
3. The **farmer** went to the field by _____.
4. The **children** play by _____.
5. The **boy** asked _____ the question.
6. **We** cooked _____ some chicken.
7. The **mule** wanted to be by _____.
8. **You** _____ can read this lesson.
9. **They** got _____ cups of coffee.
10. **I** don't know the answer _____.
11. Please do the exercises _____.
12. This **school** _____ is not big, but it has many class-rooms.
13. **I** answered the letter _____.
14. Can **John** lift the desk by _____?
15. I have to give **Miss Morgan** _____ this book.

# Conversation

*Answer the following questions, using complete sentences:*

1. What did the old woman eat?
2. Did she spend a lot of money?
3. Where did she hide her bag of money?
4. Who cooked supper?
5. Where did the old woman go after supper?
6. Did the first servant girl wash the horse's back?
7. Did the old woman pick some apples?
8. Where did the second girl hide?
9. Did the apple tree tell the truth?

10. Did the old woman get her money from the second girl?
11. When do people eat supper—in the morning or in the evening?
12. Some of the school's chalk is in this classroom. Where is the rest of it?
13. Do you have time to study in the evening?
14. Are you tired of apples?
15. Are you going home after a time?
16. Can you carry the blackboard away?
17. Is it a wet day?
18. Are you holding something in your hand?
19. When did you go up the street?
20. What did you pass by when you came to school today?

## Write or Tell

*A Lonely Place*

*When I Have a Bag of Gold*

## Pronunciation

| / æ / | / ɑ / | / ŋ / |
|---|---|---|
| have | lots | running |
| bag | wash | washing |
| back | want | thinking |
| after | not | thank |

| | |
|---|---|
| / ɑ / | Lots of boys do not want to wash. |
| / æ / | She had the bag on her back. |
| / ŋ / | The singing girl was washing the eating horse. |
| / æ, ɑ / | I do not have to wash its back. |

# Unit 4

# Crazy

Once there was a little boy who forgot everything.

One rainy morning his father wanted to go to the city, but he didn't have a wagon. He called his son and said, "Go to your uncle, boy, and get his wagon for me." On a piece of paper, he wrote, "PLEASE SEND ME YOUR WAGON," because he knew his son forgot things.

"Give that piece of paper to your uncle. Don't forget, boy. Don't forget."

"Don't forget, boy. Don't forget," the boy repeated.

The uncle lived far away and on the way the boy lost his piece of paper. He couldn't find it in the mud. He stood near a tree beside the road. He thought, "What does my father want? What did he say? I'm far from my uncle's house, and it's raining. I think I'll go home." So he walked along the road toward his house.

"My father said, 'Don't forget, boy. Don't forget.' "

He was repeating this sentence when he met a man on the road. The man was running because he did not have his umbrella.

"Don't forget, boy. Don't forget," said the little boy.

The man thought the boy was mocking him. He grabbed him by the ear and said, "Say you're sorry you did it, or I'll whip you."

"I'm sorry."

"You learn politeness, or I'll wash your mouth with soap," said the man, and he let go of the boy and went along the road.

"Wash with soap," repeated the boy.

Just then the boy saw an old woman slip in the mud and fall down. Her hands and clothes got muddy.

When he came near the old woman, the boy was still talking to himself. "Wash with soap," he said.

The old woman got out of the slippery mud. She thought the boy was mocking her. She shook her finger at him.

"I want to push *you* in, but I'm too old," she said.

The boy went on. "I want to push *you* in, but I'm too old," he repeated.

He came to a fisherman by the river. "I want to push *you* in, but I'm too old," he said.

The fisherman grabbed him and looked at him from head to foot.

"What's your name, little boy?"

"Don't forget, boy. Don't forget," said the boy.

"What shall I do with you?"

"Wash with soap," said the boy.

"I want to push you in the river!"

"I want to push *you* in, but I'm too old," the boy said.

"You're crazy!" said the fisherman and gave him a push. "Go home to your pa."

The boy ran along. "You're crazy," he repeated to himself. When he came to his home, his father ·was waiting for him.

"Didn't you get the wagon?" asked the man.

"Don't forget, boy. Don't forget."

"Well, where is it?" asked the man. "What shall I do without a wagon?"

"Wash with soap."

"I'll have to get it myself," said the man. He pushed his son into the house. "Go in and put on dry pants and a dry shirt," he said.

"I want to push *you* in, but I'm too old," said the boy.

"Boy, do you want a whipping?"

"You're crazy!" said the boy.

Do you think he got a whipping?

## Vocabulary

| | | | |
|---|---|---|---|
| against | to grab | to push | sorry |
| crazy | to mock | shirt | toward |
| ear | mouth | to slip | wagon |
| to fall | mud | slippery | to whip |
| finger | muddy | soap | whipping |
| fisherman, fishermen | pants | somewhere | |

## Idioms

to fall down
far away
far from (somewhere)
from head to foot
to let go of (something)

to look at (something)
to be sorry
to wait for (something)
to walk along

## Related Words

crazy (adj.)
crazily (adv.)
craziness (noun)

to fall (verb)
fall (noun)

to grab (verb)
grab (noun)

to mock (verb)
mockery (noun)

to push (verb)
push (noun)

to whip (verb)
whip (noun)
whipping (noun)

## Opposites

to fall down—to get up
to push—to pull
sorry—glad
toward—away from

## Structure

### I. THE PAST PROGRESSIVE TENSE WITH <u>WHEN</u>

*From your reading:*

He **was repeating** this sentence **when he met** a man on the road.

**When he came** to his home, his father **was waiting** for him.

A. *In a sentence using the past progressive tense with <u>when</u>, two actions are described. One action happened in a longer time and the other happened in a shorter time. The longer action started before the shorter action and continued to happen at the same time as the shorter action.*

*The shorter action is described with the simple past tense and the longer action with the past progressive tense. The word <u>when</u> is used just before the part of the sentence describing the shorter action.*

Structure (continued)

> *Either part may be put first in the sentence without changing the meaning. If the part with <u>when</u> is put first, a comma is used after the first part.*

He was eating dinner **when the dog began to bark.**
**When the dog began to bark,** he was eating dinner.

She was crying **when he returned home.**
**When he returned home,** she was crying.

They were dancing under the trees **when the rain started.**
**When the rain started,** they were dancing under the trees.

**B.** *In this exercise, connect the sentences in each pair, changing the underlined verbs to the past progressive tense. Sometimes <u>when</u> will be used at the beginning of the sentence and sometimes in the middle of the sentence.*

> *Example: The boy walked along the road. He saw a wagon.*
> *The boy was walking along the road when he saw a wagon.*

1. Mary **studied** English. Her father came home.
2. We **played** tennis. The rain began.
3. The children **slept.** Their mother came into the bedroom.
4. The boy **went** to school. He remembered the exercise.
5. He **ate** an apple. He cut his finger.
6. I **looked** for my pencil. The teacher spoke.
7. We **talked** about you. You came into the room.
8. We didn't see them. They **threw** the books.
9. John **read** a book. His friends came.
10. We **didn't look.** The small boy took the chalk.

## II. PREPOSITIONS: <u>IN</u>, <u>AT</u>, <u>ON</u>, <u>BY</u>, <u>BESIDE</u>, <u>AGAINST</u>, <u>FROM</u>, <u>NEAR</u>

*From your reading:*

The boy saw an old woman slip **in** the mud.
She shook her finger **at** him.

**On** a piece of paper, he wrote a note.
He came to a fisherman **by** the river.
He grabbed him **by** the ear.
He stood **beside** the road.
His family said it was **against** his nature to remember things.
He stood **beside** the road and leaned **against** a tree.
"I'm far **from** my uncle's house."
He came **near** the old woman.

A. *Read these sentences. Make other sentences using the same prepositions:*

1. We were **in** the classroom.
2. She is **at** the door.
3. The book is **on** the desk.
4. The house was **by** the river.
5. The mule was standing **beside** the tree.
6. He put his chair **against** the wall.
7. He lives far **from** the school.
8. She lives **near** the school.

B. *Read the following sentences, using the better preposition in each:*

*Example: Put the book [on/in] the desk, please.*
        *Put the book **on** the desk, please.*

1. John lived [in/on] a small town.
2. He put the table [at/against] the wall.
3. The woman is sitting [on/at] the table.
4. I can read his book because he is [at/beside] me.
5. My brother lives [beside/near] me. I can speak to him from my window.
6. My friend lives [beside/near] me. I can walk to his house in ten minutes.
7. My country is [far from/against] your country.
8. He put his hands [near/against] the fire to warm them.
9. The boy sat with his back [on/against] the wall.
10. [Beside/On] the door stood a little old man.
11. The house is [by/at] the street.

**Structure** (continued)

12. We live [in/on] South Street.
13. Please come sit [by/against] the window with me.
14. [At/On] the desk are three books.
15. London is not very [near/beside] here.

# Conversation

*Answer these questions, using complete sentences:*

1. What did the little boy always do?
2. What did the man give his son?
3. Did the uncle live near the boy's home?
4. What did the man on the road forget?
5. Why did the man grab the boy's ear?
6. Did the old woman grab the boy?
7. Who fell into the river?
8. Who was by the river?
9. When the boy came to his home, who was waiting for him?
10. Were the boy's clothes dry when he came home?
11. When is the road slippery?
12. When a person falls down, what does he do?
13. What usually pulls a wagon?
14. How many wheels does a wagon have?
15. Do you like to wait for people?
16. Do you remember yesterday's vocabulary?
17. Is it polite to mock people?
18. When you forget your book, what do you do?
19. Is your shirt blue?
20. Is there a wagon near the school?

## Write or Tell

*A Crazy Story*

*Something I Forgot*

## Dictation

*Listen to, repeat, and then write each of the following sentences:*

A boy was walking along the road when he met an old woman. She slipped and fell down in the mud. Her hands were muddy, and her clothes were muddy, too. Then he met a fisherman beside the river. The man thought the boy was mocking him, and he wanted to whip him. "I'm sorry," said the boy, and the fisherman let him go.

## Pronunciation

| / ow / | / g / | / k / |
|--------|-------|-------|
| go | go | crazy |
| road | get | mock |
| soap | grab | ask |
| home | forget | clothes |

/ ow /  Let's go home along the road.

/ g /  Go get the big girl.

/ k /  They mocked his crazy clothes.

/ g, k /  Don't forget to grab the crazy boy and ask him to go to school.

# Unit 5

# Death and the Old Man

There was once a mean old man. He was mean when he was young, and he was still mean when he was old. No one came to visit him, and he lived alone on his farm. Sometimes when he wanted to be mean, he threw sticks at his chickens, but he was too old to hit them.

One day the old man was sitting on his porch when he saw someone walking up the road to his house. The stranger walked to the porch and stood on the steps.

"Good evening," said the old man. "I don't know you. Are you new in this place?"

---

Adapted from *Journal of American Folklore,* "Jack-O-My Lantern."

"Good evening, old man," said the stranger. "No, I'm not new here. I visit often. My name is Death."

The old man sat up in his chair. "Well, Death. I didn't expect you. What business do you have here?"

"It's strange that people don't expect me," said Death. "*You* are my business, old man. I've come for you. Put on your hat and come with me."

The old man didn't want to go with Death. "Thank you very much for the invitation, Death," he said. "It was good of you to come to see me. But I prefer to live. I want more time. I have a big field of corn to take care of. Come again in two or three years."

Death didn't have time to talk about it. He had lots of people to visit. "Well," he said, "go take care of your corn. I'll come back next Saturday. Will you be ready to go with me then?"

The old man didn't answer. Death went away and the old man began smoking his pipe.

Three or four days went by. On Saturday morning the old man was in his cornfield. He was pulling weeds when he heard a noise in the corn. He looked up. There was Death.

"Come on, old man," Death said. "I'm busy this morning. I can't wait a long time for you."

"Good morning, Death," the old man said. "It's a fine day. Come and help me pull weeds."

When he heard these words, Death frowned angrily. "Now listen to me, old man," he said. "I have a lot of work to do. I can't keep coming here for you."

"Death," said the old man, "give me some more time. I have to take care of this cornfield. And I plan to hit one of those chickens of mine with a stick before I die. Come back another time."

"All right, I'll come again," Death said.

"You do that," said the old man.

Death went away and the man started pulling weeds. He lived as always. He didn't think about getting ready for Death. Winter came and went.

One spring day the old man was in his cornfield again. Death came to visit him there. "Come on, old man," he said. "You have to go with me this time."

"Good morning, Death," the old man said. "Sit down and rest. Do you want something to eat?"

"I'm busy," said Death. "Get your hat."

"I don't like seeing you here so often," said the old man. "Next time send me a letter. Perhaps I'll come then."

Death was tired of the old man. "All right," he said, and he went away.

The old man got older and older. He became deaf and blind. One morning he got a letter from Death, but he couldn't read it. When the old man wrote no answer, Death came once more to visit him. He was very angry.

"You tricked me too many times, old man. I don't want you now."

The old man became older than the oldest trees, but he didn't die. Death left him alone. People say that he never died. He just disappeared.

## Vocabulary

| | | | |
|---|---|---|---|
| angry | deaf | mean | still |
| angrily | to disappear | pipe | strange |
| to become | to expect | porch | stranger |
| blind | to frown | shall | weed |
| contraction | just | to smoke | will |
| corn | to leave | step | |

## Idioms

| | |
|---|---|
| as always | to leave (something) alone |
| to come back | to sit up |
| to get ready for (something) | to take care of (something) |
| It's good of you to come. | |

## Related Words

angry (adj.)
anger (noun)
angrily (adv.)

deaf (adj.)
deafness (noun)

to disappear (verb)
disappearance (noun)

to expect (verb)
expectation (noun)

to frown (verb)
frown (noun)

step (noun)
to step (verb)

strange (adj.)
strangely (adv.)
strangeness (noun)
stranger (noun)

mean (adj.)
meanness (noun)

to smoke (verb)
smoke (noun)
smoky (adj.)

## Opposites

to disappear—to appear
to frown—to smile
strange—familiar

## Structure

### I. INFINITIVES AND GERUNDS AS OBJECTS OF <u>BEGIN</u>, <u>START</u>, <u>LIKE</u>, <u>PREFER</u>, <u>PLAN</u>

*From your reading:*

The old man **began smoking** his pipe.
The man **started pulling** weeds.
"I don't **like seeing** you come here so often."
"I **prefer to live**."
"I **plan to hit** one of those chickens."

A. *Some verbs, for example,* <u>*begin*</u>, <u>*start*</u>, <u>*like*</u>, <u>*prefer*</u>, *and* <u>*plan*</u>, *may take either infinitives or gerunds as objects.*

**to** + verb = infinitive (**to read**)
verb + **ing** = gerund (**reading**)

**Structure** (continued)

*Read these sentences:*

She **likes pulling** weeds. = She **likes to pull** weeds.
He **prefers picking** flowers. = He **prefers to pick** flowers.
They **began talking** loudly. = They **began to talk** loudly.
Are you **planning to go** now? = Are you **planning on going** now?

REVIEW NOTE: *We usually use* <u>on</u> *after* <u>plan</u> *before a gerund:*
*They* <u>plan on singing</u> *all night. He* <u>plans on going</u> *early.*

B. **In the following exercise, give each sentence first with**
   **the gerund and then with the infinitive of the verb in**
   **parentheses:**

*Example: The man began ＿＿ (eat) ＿＿.*
         *The man began eating.*
         *The man began to eat.*

1. I like ＿＿ (play) ＿＿ football.
2. We plan ＿＿ (go) ＿＿ to Paris next year.
3. Does he like ＿＿ (ride) ＿＿ his horse?
4. I don't like ＿＿ (see) ＿＿ him here so often.
5. He started ＿＿ (smoke) ＿＿ his pipe.
6. I prefer ＿＿ (read) ＿＿ history books.
7. The old man began ＿＿ (pull) ＿＿ the grass.
8. When will you start ＿＿ (study) ＿＿ the lesson?
9. He began ＿＿ (frown) ＿＿ when he became angry.
10. The boys planned ＿＿ (hide) ＿＿ from their mother.
11. The mule didn't like ＿＿ (work) ＿＿ in the morning.
12. I prefer ＿＿ (stand) ＿＿ in a bus.
13. He started ＿＿ (lift) ＿＿ the table, but it was too heavy.
14. I plan ＿＿ (go) ＿＿ to bed early tonight.
15. Did she begin ＿＿ (cry) ＿＿ in the theater?

16. Has she started _____ (do) _____ the housework?
17. The farmer liked ~~to liv~~ (live) _living_
18. The stranger preferred _____ (take) _____ the old man with him.
19. Didn't you begin _____ (do) _____ the exercise last night?
20. He plans _____ (sit) _____ in the back of the class.

## II. THE FUTURE TENSE

*From your reading:*

"I'll come back next Saturday."
"Will you be ready to go then?"

A. *With I and we, we may use <u>will</u> or <u>shall</u> to form the future tense. With <u>all</u> others (<u>you</u>, <u>he</u>, <u>she</u>, <u>it</u>, <u>they</u>) we use <u>will</u>.*

**I shall expect** you tomorrow.
**We shall plan** to come to the play.
**He will smoke** his pipe.
**She will be** angry.
**The classroom will be** empty at six o'clock.

*In conversation we usually use the contraction of <u>shall</u> or <u>will</u>.*

**I'll give** you my book later.
**They'll hide** under the table.

B. *To ask a question in the future tense, we put the word <u>will</u> or <u>shall</u> before the subject.*

**Shall I expect** you tomorrow?
**Will he smoke** the cigarette?

C. *Use <u>shall</u> or <u>will</u> in the following sentences. After pronouns, use the contraction of <u>will</u> as you speak:*

1. He _____ try to hit a chicken.
2. I think I _____ go home now.
3. I expect that he _____ go with me.
4. She _____ stay in the classroom.

Structure (continued)

5. We _____ all become old.
6. Perhaps they _____ go together.
7. Mary _____ wash the dishes.
8. I think it _____ rain tomorrow.
9. The horse _____ do the work.
10. I _____ be twenty years old next week.
11. _____ she expect us to go home in the rain?
12. _Shall_ I take a pencil, too?
13. _will_ they prefer going to the park?
14. _will_ Mr. Brown plan to visit our class?
15. William _will_ fill the pitcher with water.

# Conversation

*Answer the following questions, using complete sentences:*

1. Where did the old man live?
2. Did someone live with him?
3. Was he a kind man?
4. Who was the stranger who came to visit him?
5. What did the stranger want?
6. Was the stranger deaf?
7. Where was the old man sitting when the stranger came the first time?
8. Did the old man smoke cigarettes?
9. Why couldn't he read the letter?
10. How old did he become?
11. Do you smoke a pipe?
12. Do you expect to go home soon?
13. Can a deaf person see?
14. Do you have a porch on your house?
15. Did you ever see a man disappear?
16. Do you like to take care of a garden?
17. Is it good to have weeds in a garden?

18. When do you usually get ready for school?
19. Is it better to leave an angry dog alone?
20. Are you still sitting at your desk?

## Write or Tell

*My Favorite Garden*

*A Strange Story*

## Dictation

*Listen to, repeat, and then write each of the following sentences:*

The old man lived alone on his farm because he was so mean. He liked working in his cornfield and throwing sticks at his chickens. He didn't want to go with Death. Perhaps he finally died or perhaps he disappeared. We'll never know.

## Pronunciation

| / ɔ / | / h / |
|-------|-------|
| saw | he |
| often | hit |
| talk | house |
| all | here |
| always | hat |
| call | heard |

/ ɔ /   We all often saw them talk.

/ h /   He heard us here in the house.

# Unit 6

# The Son Who Went
# to College

A farmer and his wife had a son who liked to study. They loved him very much, so they saved money for him and sent him to a college in the city. In seven years, he finished his studies and came home. His old mother and father were proud of the boy who could read books.

One morning the mother went outdoors to milk the cows. There was a new young cow that was very wild. When the old woman tried to milk her, she kicked.

---

Adapted from Zora Neale Hurston, "The Son Who Went to College."

When the cow kept on kicking, the woman called to her husband, "Come out and help me with the cow." The old man went out and tried to hold the cow, but the cow kept on jumping and kicked him.

Then he said, "We don't have to worry about her. We have a son who went to college. He has studied many things and has learned a lot. He knows how to take care of a wild cow. I'll call him."

The old man called his son and told him about the cow. The boy came out of the house and looked at her for a time. Then he said, "Don't worry about this cow. Before she can kick, she has to bend her back. We have to make her back straight."

The father said, "I don't understand, Son, but, of course, you've been to college. You know more than your mother and father. Straighten the cow's back. We'll be very happy."

The son put on his gold eyeglasses. He studied the cow from head to foot. Then he said, "We need a weight for her back. That will straighten it."

"What do you want for a weight, Son?" asked the father.

"Oh, any weight, Pa—any weight that's very heavy."

"All right, but where will we get a weight, Son?"

"*You* get on her back, Pa. You're heavy."

"Son, you were at school a long time. You've forgotten that it's hard to sit on a cow, and I'm getting old, you know."

"But, Pa, I'll tie your feet together under her. Then you won't fall off. Please get on now."

"All right, Son. You want me to get on the cow, and I'll get on her. You know more than I do—I think."

They tied the cow to a tree, and the old man climbed onto her back. It was hard for him to climb. The boy tied his father's feet together under the cow. But, again, when the old woman tried to milk her, the animal began to kick. She kicked and jumped, and the old man began asking to get down. He kept calling to his son, "Cut the rope, boy! Cut the rope! I want to get down."

The boy didn't cut the rope around his father's feet. He cut the rope that tied the cow to the tree.

Then she began to run. She ran across the field with the man on her back. She ran through the woods. The old man couldn't do a thing to stop her.

Finally, the cow ran down a little dirt road. There was a neighbor woman walking along the road. She was surprised to see the farmer on the cow's back. She asked, "Where are you going, Brother? Why are you riding on that cow?"

"Only the Lord, my son, and this cow know," he said.

## Vocabulary

| | | | |
|---|---|---|---|
| across | glasses, eyeglasses | proud | to surprise |
| action | heavy | to ride | under |
| around | to jump | to save | weight |
| to bend | the Lord | straight | wild |
| to continue | to love | to straighten | to worry |
| to finish | neighbor | studies | |

## Idioms

to fall off
to get old
to keep on (doing something)
to take place

to tell (someone) about (something)
to worry about (something)

## Related Words

| | | |
|---|---|---|
| across (adv.) | proud (adj.) | to surprise (verb) |
| to cross (verb) | pride (noun) | surprise (noun) |
| | proudly (adv.) | surprised (adj.) |

heavy (adj.)
heavily (adv.)
heaviness (noun)

to ride (verb)
ride (noun)
rider (noun)

weight (noun)
to weigh (verb)
weighty (adj.)

to love (verb)
love (noun)

to study (verb)
study (noun)
studies (noun)

to worry (verb)
worry (noun)

## Opposites

to finish—to begin, to start
heavy—light
to love—to hate
straight—crooked
under—over
wild—tame

## Structure

### I. THE PRESENT PERFECT TENSE

*From your reading:*

"He **has studied** many things and **has learned** a lot."
"You **have been** to college."
"You've **forgotten** that it's hard to sit on a cow."

A. *The present perfect tense is used in two ways. It may describe an action that took place in the past and is now completed, or it may describe an action that started in the past and is still continuing in the present. If the action described with the present perfect tense is now completed, the time of the action ("when I was young," "last month," "two years ago") is not indicated.*

*Simple Past—Time Given:*

He studied many things when he was in school.
He learned a lot three years ago.

**Structure** (continued)

> *Present Perfect—No Time Given:*
> He has studied many things.
> He has learned a lot.

*If the present perfect tense is used for an action that began in the past and is still continuing in the present, the time ("since I was young," "since last month," "this month," "for two years") can be indicated.*

> If I am still studying English now:
> I've studied English for two years.
> I have studied English for two years.
>
> If I am not studying English now:
> I have studied English.
> I've studied English.
> I studied English for two years.

**B. Read these sentences after your teacher:**

1. I've enjoyed his stories for a long time.
2. I've seen her often this year.
3. You've gone to the store twice this week.
4. You've studied a lot since the last test.
5. She's read every book in the house since winter began.
6. He's worked on the farm for four years.
7. We've climbed that tree many times.
8. We've seen the movie.
9. They've eaten apples since they had teeth.
10. They've saved a lot of money in the last two years.

**C. In the following sentences, use the present perfect tense when possible and the past tense when not:**

*Example: The teacher _____ (explain) _____ the lesson.*
*The teacher has explained the lesson.*

1. She _____ (explain) _____ it yesterday.
2. I _____ (play) _____ the piano three years ago.

3. She ____ (study) ____ piano.
4. The farmer's son ____ (finish) ____ his studies.
5. He ____ (finish) ____ them last year.
6. We ____ (save) ____ a lot of money to buy a house.
7. Last year we ____ (buy) ____ a radio.
8. I ____ (finish) ____ studying at ten o'clock last night.
9. Their son ____ (study) ____ English.
10. I can't find my pen. I ____ (look) ____ for it since yesterday.
11. John _has_ (come) ____ to class. He ____ (come) ____ ten minutes ago.
12. He _has_ (be) ____ late every day this year. He _was_ (be) ____ always late last year, too.
13. We _have_ (not finish) ____ this lesson.
14. I ____ (walk) ____ by the river yesterday.
15. I _love_ (walk) ____ there very often.

## II. <u>THAT</u> AS SUBJECT OF ADJECTIVE CLAUSES

*From your reading:*

*He cut the rope that tied the cow.*
*There was a cow that was very wild.*
*"We can use any weight that's very heavy."*

A. **You have learned that <u>who</u> is used only for people. <u>That</u> is used for people, animals, and things.**

B. **Connect the following sentences, using the relative pronoun <u>that</u>:**

Example: *They are the glasses. They were on his nose.*
      *They are the glasses **that** were on his nose.*

1. They saved paper in a box. It was in their house.
2. She worried about the child. He was riding the cow.
3. The little boy likes to climb the tree. It is in the garden.
4. The farmer held the rope. It was tied to the cow.
5. He is the boy. He went home early.

**Structure** (continued)

6. Mary has a cat. It is very wild.
7. She is the neighbor. She was walking along the road.
8. Cows are animals. They have four feet.
9. She passed the tree. It was full of apples.
10. There is the chimney. It has a bag of gold in it.

# Conversation

*Answer the following questions, using complete sentences:*

1. Where did the son go to college?
2. How long did he study?
3. What did the son put on?
4. Why did he want a weight?
5. What did the cow do?
6. Did the father want to sit on the cow's back?
7. Did he fall off? Why or why not?
8. What did they tie the cow to?
9. Where did the cow run?
10. Who was surprised? Why?
11. What are you holding in your hand?
12. Do you know many of your neighbors?
13. Is the road near the school straight?
14. Are dogs usually wild?
15. What is something that you are proud of?
16. Do you like surprises?
17. Is the sun very far away?
18. Do you like to save old things?
19. Do parents usually love their children?
20. Have we finished reading the story?

# Write or Tell

### The Son's Story

("My parents were farmers, but they sent me to the city to college. I finished my studies in seven years," etc.)

## Dictation

*Listen to, repeat, and then write each of the following sentences:*

A farmer and his wife had a son who went to college. He finished his studies in seven years and came home. The father thought the boy knew more than he himself. When his son told him to climb onto the cow, he did it. The old man has been on the cow ever since.

## Pronunciation

| / ow / | / ɔ / | / w / |
|--------|-------|-------|
| hold | call | want |
| old | across | was |
| rope | always | wife |
| know | talk | woman |

/ ow /    I know the old man will hold the rope.

/ ɔ /    We always saw him across the street.

/ w /    That woman was his wife.

/ ow, ɔ /    He always talks about the old rope that he saw.

# Unit 7

# The Cure

Once there was a sick old man who had rheumatism and couldn't walk. He hadn't walked for ten years. All day he sat in front of his house and thought about his rheumatism. At night his family carried him to bed.

"Won't I ever walk again?" he asked. His family didn't think so.

One day, when he was sitting in his chair looking at the road, a boy that came along stopped to talk to him.

"Do you know the old cemetery, which is down this road?" asked the boy.

---

Adapted from Richard Chase, "The Cure."

"Yes, I do," said the old man.

"People say the Devil and the Lord are there. They say that they are dividing the souls," said the boy. "Do you believe it?"

"Perhaps yes and perhaps no," answered the old man.

"Nobody will go there at night. Everybody I know is afraid. Nobody will go there on a dark night, or on a clear one, either. Aren't you afraid, too?"

"I'm not afraid," said the old man, "but I can't walk so far."

The boy became excited. "Will you go there with me?" he asked. "I'll carry you on my back."

"Of course I'll go," said the old man. They planned on going that same night.

That day two thieves came to town. They usually stole together. This time the first one planned to steal a sheep, and the second planned to steal some ears of corn. They decided to meet at night in the cemetery.

When the thief with the corn went to the cemetery, his friend wasn't there. The thief put the corn on the ground and began to divide the ears. "I'll take this one; he can have that one. I'll take this ear; he can have that ear."

When the boy picked up the old man, he found that he was very heavy, so he soon put him down on the road. "Aren't you going to carry me all the way?" asked the old man. "I can't walk, you know." So the boy picked him up again and started on.

After a time the boy came along with the old man on his back. They heard the thief say, "I'll take this one; he can have that one," but it was too dark to see anyone.

The thief heard the boy and thought it was his friend with the sheep.

"Is he fat?" he yelled.

The boy's hair stood up on his head. He threw the old man to the ground and said, "Fat or thin, you can have him!" Then he turned around and ran as fast as he could run.

He stopped running when he came to the old man's house. There was a light on the porch, and he saw the old man, sitting in his chair, smoking a cigar!

"Why are you so slow?" called the old man.

That old man never had rheumatism again. He was cured. And the boy never went to the cemetery again, day or night.

## Vocabulary

| | | | |
|---|---|---|---|
| to believe | the Devil | ground | soul |
| cemetery | to divide | nobody | to steal |
| cigar | everybody | rheumatism | strong |
| clear | excited | sheep | thief |
| cure | fast | sick | thin |
| dark | fat | slow | |

## Idioms

as fast as one can

to come along

to be cured

too dark to see

day or night

ear of corn

in front of (something)

to pick (something) up

to put (something) down

to think about (something)

to turn around

## Related Words

to believe (verb)
belief (noun)
believable (adj.)

cigar (noun)
cigarette (noun)

cloudy (adj.)
cloud (noun)
cloudiness (noun)

dark (adj.)
dark (noun)
darkness (noun)
to darken (verb)

excited (adj.)
to excite (verb)
excitement (noun)
exciting (adj.)

sick (adj.)
sickly (adj.)
sickness (noun)

strong (adj.)
strength (noun)
to strengthen (verb)

# Opposites

dark—light
fast—slow
fat—thin
in front of—in back of
to pick up—to put down
sick—well
strong—weak

# Structure

## I. ADVERBS OF FREQUENCY

*From your reading:*

"Won't I **ever** walk again?"
They **usually** stole together.
That old man **never** had rheumatism again.

*A. Some common frequency words are ever, never, always,*
*sometimes, often, usually, and seldom.*

*Ever is used only in negative statements, but is used in both*
*affirmative and negative questions.*

*Read these sentences:*

Does he **ever** go there?
    Yes, **sometimes** he does.
    Yes, **sometimes** he goes there.
    No, he **never** does.
    No, he **never** goes there.
    No, he doesn't **ever** go there.

*B. Use a frequency word in each of the following questions.*
*Give a short answer and a long answer, each with a fre-*
*quency word.*

Structure (continued)

> *Example: Did they visit him at home?*
> *Did they **sometimes** visit him at home?*
> *Yes, sometimes they did.*
> *Yes, sometimes they visited him at home.*
> *No, they never did.*
> *No, they never visited him at home.*
> *No, they didn't ever visit him at home.*

1. Will he ever have rheumatism again?
2. Did the old man smoke cigars?
3. Will it be dark at six o'clock?
4. Has Mary written us a letter?
5. Does someone erase the blackboard?
6. Will we have chicken for dinner?
7. Won't the old man ever walk again?
8. Won't they sit on the porch?
9. Will you write in your notebook?
10. Did the sun disappear?
11. Won't he become angry?
12. Won't you go with them?
13. Will your neighbor ever come to visit you?
14. Do you ever write as fast as you can?
15. Can you hold a pencil in your hand?

## II. THE RELATIVE PRONOUNS <u>WHO</u>, <u>WHOM</u>, <u>WHICH</u>, AND <u>THAT</u>

*From your reading:*

There was **an old man who had rheumatism.**
Everybody **whom I know** is afraid.
Do you know **the old cemetery, which is down this road?**
**A boy that came along** stopped to talk.

### A. *Read these sentences:*

The old man is on the porch.
The old man **who has rheumatism** is on the porch.

The old man **whom you know** is on the porch.
The old man **that John** saw is on the porch.

The book is on the table.
    The book, **which is green**, is on the table.
    The book **that we read** is on the table.

B. **Who** is the subject in its clause; <u>whom</u> is the object in its clause. **Who** and <u>whom</u> are used only for persons.

    He is the boy **who has the book.**
    He is the boy **whom you know.**

C. **Which** and **that** are either subjects or objects of the clauses they are in.

    The other book, **which I wanted**, is very interesting.
    These books, **which are old and dirty**, are very interesting.

    Here is the chair **that is the biggest.**
    Here is the chair that **John sat on.**

*That is used for persons, animals, or things.* <u>Which</u> *is used for animals or things, not for persons.*

D. *Use* <u>who</u>, *whom, which, or that in the following sentences:*

1. She is the girl _**who**_ is afraid of the dark.
2. That is the pencil _____ I found yesterday.
3. The boy _____ we saw is John.
4. It was a big cigar _____ he smoked.
5. He is the thief _____ stole the sheep.
6. The sheep _**that**_ he stole was white.
7. Everybody _**that**_ heard the thief ran away.
8. There is the mule _**that**_ walked away from the boy.
9. I told this story to a girl _**who**_ believed it.
10. He visited the cemetery _**that**_ is down the road.
11. Matthew, _**who**_ we met on the street, is a student.
12. The boy _**who**_ was with him is also a student.
13. Nobody _**that**_ is in this class is absent today.
14. The chair _**that**_ the teacher uses is in the corner.
15. Bring me the piece of chalk _**that**_ is on the desk.

## Conversation

*Answer the following questions, using complete sentences:*

1. Why couldn't the old man walk?
2. Where did he usually sit?
3. Who stopped to talk to him?
4. What was down the road?
5. How many thieves came to town?
6. What did they plan to steal?
7. What did the second thief count in the cemetery?
8. Who did the boy think was there?
9. How did the old man go to the cemetery?
10. How did he leave it?
11. Do you know everybody in this class?
12. Are there many sheep in your country?
13. Are you excited when you take a trip?
14. Do you believe this story?
15. Can you divide nine by three? Eight by three?
16. Do you like to smoke cigars?
17. Are you afraid of the dark?
18. Can strong men play football? Can sick men?
19. Can we see a soul?
20. What color is the hair of old people?

## Write or Tell

*A Dark Night*

*An Exciting Story*

## Dictation

*Listen to, repeat, and then write each of the following sentences:*

The old man with rheumatism sat in front of his house. One day a boy told him about a cemetery down the road. He said that the Devil and the Lord were there. The boy carried the old man to the cemetery in the dark. A thief yelled, "Is he fat?" and the boy dropped the old man to the ground. They both ran away, but the old man ran faster than the boy.

# Pronunciation

| / iy / | / f / | / v / |
|---|---|---|
| he | thief | of |
| believe | family | thieves |
| thief | first | divide |
| evening | fat | never |

| | |
|---|---|
| / iy / | He believes he saw the thief. |
| / f / | My family is afraid of the first fat thief. |
| / v / | We have never divided with the thieves. |
| / f, v / | The thieves have never been afraid of the first family. |

# Unit 8

# Hans the Butterman

When New York City was not very big, there was a market on the East River. On market day all the farmers came there to sell their vegetables, butter and eggs, and fruit. They laughed and talked together, so no one could hear the river that ran beside them.

But Hans the butterman sat without a smile. He sold pounds of butter from a table beside him. Many people said that his butter wasn't the right weight. They said that his rolls of butter didn't weigh as much as a pound.

Once the weighmaster came walking down the road. He was

Adapted from M. Jagendorf, "Hans the Butter Man."

looking for people who did not sell the full weight. Someone told him, "Watch Hans, the butterman."

Hans had good eyes. He saw the weighmaster and quickly put a heavy piece of gold into the first roll of butter, between the butter and its cover.

A captain was standing beside Hans's table, and he had seen Hans put the piece of gold into the roll. He stood at Hans's side when the weighmaster came up to him.

"Good morning," said the weighmaster.

"Good morning," said Hans. "I think that you are looking for farmers who trick the people of our town."

"I am," said the weighmaster. "Someone told me that your rolls of butter don't weigh a full pound."

"Oh, yes, they do. Here, Weighmaster. Here is a roll of butter. Weigh it yourself," said Hans.

Hans took the first roll of butter and gave it to the weighmaster.

The weighmaster took his scales and put the butter onto it. The roll weighed more than a pound.

"I've made a mistake," said the weighmaster. "You are an honest man. There is enough butter in this roll."

Then the captain stood in front of Hans's table. "You are an honest man, so I want to buy some of your butter," he said. Before Hans could speak, the captain picked up the roll of butter with the piece of gold in it. "I'll take this one."

Hans's heart began beating more quickly. "No, not that one. I've sold that one to a friend of mine. Take another one."

"No, I want this one," said the captain.

"I won't sell it to you. I told you that I've sold it to a friend," said Hans.

"Don't make me angry. The weighmaster weighed this roll. Give your friend another one."

"But I want to give him this one," said Hans, who was now very uncomfortable.

"I ask you, good Weighmaster," said the captain angrily, "don't I have the right to choose the piece of butter that I want? I will pay good money for it."

"Of course you have the right, Captain," said the weighmaster. "What are you afraid of, Hans? Aren't all the rolls of butter alike? Perhaps I have to weigh all of them."

What could Hans say? What could he do? He had to smile and sell the butter to the captain. The captain gave Hans three cents for the butter.

The captain and the weighmaster walked away together.

"You punished the thief," said the weighmaster.

"No, he punished himself," said the captain, smiling.

## Vocabulary

| | | | |
|---|---|---|---|
| to add | full | modify | roll |
| alike | heart | onto | scales |
| captain | honest | order, word order | side |
| to choose | list | pound | uncomfortable |
| cover | market | to precede | weighmaster |
| enough | mistake | to punish | |

## Idioms

to come up to (something)
down the road
to make (someone) angry
to make a mistake

to pay good money for (something)
to have the right to (something, do something)

## Related Words

to choose (verb)
choice (noun)
choice (adj.)

honest (adj.)
honesty (noun)

to punish (verb)
punishment (noun)

uncomfortable (adj.)
comfort (noun)
comfortable (adj.)
discomfort (noun)

## Opposites

alike—different
honest—dishonest
into—out of
to punish—to reward
top—bottom
uncomfortable—comfortable

## Structure

### I. ADJECTIVES

*From your reading:*

New York was not very **big**.
"You are an **honest** man."
Hans was now very **uncomfortable**.

**A. *Read these sentences:***

The farmer has butter. It is **sweet, yellow butter.**
The **butter, sweet** and **yellow,** is on the table.
The **butter** is **yellow** and **sweet.**

*The words sweet and yellow modify the word butter. Sweet and yellow are adjectives.*

*Adjectives may precede a noun: sweet, yellow butter. They may follow a noun: butter, sweet and yellow. They may follow the verb to be: butter is yellow and sweet.*

**B. *Complete the sentences in this exercise with adjectives from the following list:***

| | | |
|---|---|---|
| angry – | empty | sick |
| blind | excited | strange |
| clever – | full | strong |
| dark – | mean | thin |
| deaf – | proud | true |
| dirty | sharp | wild |

**Structure (continued)**

1. It was a *true* story about *wild* animals.
2. I didn't believe the story because it wasn't *true*.
3. The man, *clever* and *thin*, told us to go away.
4. Did you wash the *dirty* dish?
5. The *strong* boy played football, but he was not _____ in school.
6. He was *proud* that he was the best player.
7. Now our classroom is *full*, but on Sunday it is *empty*.
8. The old man, *deaf* and *blind*, could not see or hear the cars.
9. One student is *sick* so he is at home today.
10. The *mean* man threw *sharp* stones at the chickens.
11. I am afraid of a *dark* night.
12. Mary can wear this dress because she is *thin*.


## II. ADVERBS

*From your reading:*

He **quickly** put a piece of gold into the roll of butter.
Hans's heart beat **quickly**.
"I ask you," said the captain **angrily**.

### A. *Read these sentences:*

I understand adverbs. I understand adverbs **now**.
The girl ran. The girl ran **away**.
He opened the window. He opened the window **quietly**.

*The words now, away, and quietly modify the verbs in these*

*sentences. Now, away, and quietly are adverbs.*

*Sometimes an adverbial phrase is used instead of an adverb.*

I understand adverbs **after much study.**
The girl ran **down the road.**
He opened the window **without a noise.**

B. *Adverbs (or adverbial phrases) of time may answer the question,* When?

**When** are you going to go home?

I am going to go home **after school.**

**When** did you see the horse?

I saw the horse **yesterday.**

*When a question is not asked, and another emphasis is wanted, the adverb of time may be placed at the beginning of the sentence.*

**Yesterday** I saw the horse.

C. *Adverbs (or adverbial phrases) of place may answer the question,* Where?

**Where** are you going?

I am going **outdoors.**

**Where** did your brother go?

He went **into the field.**

D. *Adverbs (or adverbial phrases) of manner may answer the question,* How?

**How** did the children sing?

They sang **well.**

**How** did he eat the fruit?

He ate the fruit **slowly.**

He **slowly** ate the fruit.

**Slowly,** he ate the fruit.

*Adverbs of manner are often made from adjectives by adding* ly *to the adjective:*

**slow—slowly**

*When an adjective ends in* y, *the* y *is usually changed to* i, *and* ly *is added:*

**angry—angrily**

*When an adjective ends in* ble *or* ple, *the* e *is dropped and* ly *is added:*

**comfortable—comfortably**

**simple—simply**

**Structure** (continued)

*Other examples of adverbs of manner and the adjectives from which they are made are the following:*

| | |
|---|---|
| angry—angrily | quick—quickly |
| blind—blindly | sharp—sharply |
| clever—cleverly | slow—slowly |
| excited—excitedly | strange—strangely |
| happy—happily | usual—usually |
| proud—proudly | wild—wildly |

REVIEW NOTE: <u>good</u> *is the adjective, and* <u>well</u> *is the adverb:*
He is a **good** speaker.
He speaks **well.**

E. *Sentences with adverbs may have several possible word orders. The chart on page 65 shows the easiest and most common word order.*

F. *Put the following into sentences, using the word order shown:*

1. took
   yesterday
   her book
   home
   she

2. he
   happily
   to the field
   after breakfast
   went

3. lives
   now
   she
   on the farm

4. when he saw the
      weighmaster
   put
   into the butter
   he
   the gold piece

5. his teacher
   saw
   on the street
   he
   last week

6. later
   was
   in the field
   the farmer

7. when he ran away
   yelled
   she
   angrily

8. he
   for a long time
   uncomfortably
   has sat

9. beside the
      man's feet
   sat
   this morning
   the little dog

| Subject | Verb | Object | How | Where | When |
|---|---|---|---|---|---|
| Hans the butterman | sat | | with a smile. | | |
| A captain | was standing | | | beside Hans's table. | |
| He | stood | | | at Hans's side | when the weighmaster came up to him. |
| Hans's heart | beat | | quickly. | | |
| Hans | put | the gold piece | quickly | into the butter | when he saw the weighmaster. |

**Structure (continued)**

10. the horse
    the old man
    along the road
    doesn't want to
    ride
    quickly

11. went
    the son
    to college

12. with a stick
    the cow
    is hitting
    the woman

13. up her chimney
    the old woman
    angrily
    looked

14. she
    then
    along the road
    excitedly
    ran

15. later
    found
    the servant girl
    she
    on the road

16. to the park
    we
    tomorrow
    will go

17. have to open
    we
    our books
    now

18. plans to steal
    the thief
    from the field
    tonight
    a sheep

19. walked
    he
    all night
    blindly
    along the road

20. proudly
    carried
    the old man
    into the house
    his chair

**G. In the following sentences, use adverbs made from the adjectives that are underlined:**

*Example: I think he is a proud boy. He walks so _____.*
*I think he is a proud boy. He walks so proudly.*

1. The wild cat cried _____ in the night.
2. He is blind in the dark. He walked *blindly* into the wall.
3. She was excited yesterday. She spoke *excitedly* about her visit to the farm.
4. He is a strange man. He speaks _____.
5. He became angry and threw his book *angrily* to the floor.

6. The little boy was happy when he found the piece of gold. He ran *happily* home.

7. You are a quick student. You finish your work very *quickly*

8. This is our usual lesson. We *usually* have our English lesson now.

9. Our desks are comfortable. I can sit *comfortably* here all day.

10. He is a simple man. He spoke *simply* to his son about life.

# Conversation

*Answer the following questions, using complete sentences:*

1. Where was the market where Hans sold butter?
2. Did Hans laugh very much with the other farmers?
3. What was the weighmaster looking for?
4. Who was standing beside Hans's table?
5. What did Hans put into a roll of butter? Why?
6. What did the weighmaster put the butter onto?
7. Why did the captain want to buy some butter?
8. Why didn't Hans want to sell the roll of butter?
9. How much did the captain pay for the butter?
10. How did Hans punish himself?
11. Do you sometimes make mistakes in English?
12. Are you and your friend alike?
13. Do you choose to write with a pen or a pencil?
14. Where can we find some scales?
15. Is there a market near the school?
16. What color is the cover of your book?
17. Do you have the right to go home every day?
18. Do we have enough chalk in the room?
19. Do you look up when the teacher writes on the blackboard?
20. Is your desk comfortable?

## Write or Tell

*An Uncomfortable Place to Be*

*An Honest Person I Know*

## Dictation

*Listen to, repeat, and then write each of the following sentences:*

Hans the butterman was not honest. He sold rolls of butter that didn't weigh enough. When he saw the weighmaster, he put a heavy gold piece quickly under the cover of a roll of butter. The weighmaster put that roll onto his scales, and it weighed enough. But Hans was punished when the captain bought the roll of butter with the piece of gold in it.

## Pronunciation

| / ɪ / | / ɪŋ / | / θ / |
|-------|--------|-------|
| hit | think | think |
| it | thing | thought |
| thick | pink | three |
| did | singing | cloth |
| in | ink | breath |
| sister | ring | through |

/ ɪ /   My sister did not hit it.
        I know it is in the house.

/ ɪŋ /   I think he is learning to sing.
         The thing on my finger is ink.

/ θ /   Three think the cloth is here.
        He thought his breath came through the cloth.

/ ɪ, ɪŋ /   The little boy in the pink cap stuck a pin in his finger.
            Bill thinks the ink is his.

# Unit 9

# The Lesson

Most people have a lot to learn. Many people need to learn when to talk and when not to talk. Some know a lot but tell only a little bit. Others know less and tell about half of it. There are others who know only a little and can't stop talking. They start talking and keep on talking. In the old days there was a man like this, named Sam. Sam didn't know that it is not good to tell everything. He talked about everything he knew.

One day Sam was in the woods. He cut trees there with some other workers. He was tired when he had finished work. On the

Adapted from Zora Neale Hurston, "High Walker and Bloody Bones."

way home he walked slowly. As he walked he kicked the grass with his feet. Suddenly he kicked something, and it rolled out of the grass. It was a white, dry skull. It had been there a long time.

Sam was sorry that he had kicked a skull like that. He said, "Please excuse me, skull. I'll put you back into the grass."

But before he could pick the skull up, he heard music. He looked around but didn't see anyone. He looked up and down but saw nothing. He heard someone singing, but he didn't know who it was. This is what he heard:

> *I am here and you are there;*
> *Talk too much, we'll be a pair.*

Then Sam saw that the skull on the ground was singing those words. After a time the skull became quiet. Sam said to it, "Skull, how did you come here?"

The skull answered, "My big mouth did this to me."

Sam said, "Do you know what I am going to do? I am going to tell my boss about you."

Sam was so excited that he ran from the woods. He wanted to tell everyone about the skull that he had found. Soon he found his boss and told him, "There's a skull in the woods that can talk and sing. I talked to it myself."

His boss was a man who wanted his workers to be quiet and honest. He said, "I want my workers to tell the truth. I'll go with you to see that skull. I want to see for myself what it says."

So the boss went into the woods with his worker. There Sam found the skull in the grass and showed it to his boss. You can guess what Sam wanted the skull to do.

They stood beside it a long time, but it didn't speak. Finally Sam said, "Skull, sing that song again." The skull didn't sing.

Sam said, "Skull, be my friend and talk to my boss." The skull didn't make a sound.

Then Sam's boss said to him, "I think you have been drinking whiskey, and I have to teach you a lesson. I don't want you to work for me any more. Find yourself another job." And he went away.

Again Sam was alone with the skull. Do you know what happened next? That skull began to sing:

> *I am here and you are there;*
> *Talk too much, we'll be a pair.*

Sam sat down on the ground beside the skull. He looked at it sadly and said, "Brother, why didn't you speak when my boss was here?"

"My big mouth did this to me, son," said the skull. "Your big mouth did that to you."

## Vocabulary

| | | | |
|---|---|---|---|
| any more | to excuse | to roll | suddenly |
| anyone | to form | sadly | voice |
| bit | to happen | skull | whiskey |
| boss | job | something | |
| everything | less | sound | |

## Idioms

a little bit                    to make a sound
excuse me

## Related Words

| | | |
|---|---|---|
| to excuse (verb) | to happen (verb) | suddenly (adv.) |
| excuse (noun) | happening (noun) | sudden (adj.) |
| to form (verb) | sadly (adv.) | |
| form (noun) | sad (adj.) | |
| | sadness (noun) | |

# Opposites

everything—nothing
sadly—happily
to start—to end, to finish,
to complete

# Structure

## I. THE PAST PERFECT TENSE

*From your reading:*

He **was** tired when he **had finished** work.
It **was** a white skull. It **had been** there a long time.
Sam **was** sorry that he **had kicked** a skull like that.

A. *We form the past perfect tense by adding* <u>had</u> *to the past participle of the main verb.*

**written**      **had written**

*The past perfect tense is used only when there is another verb in some other past tense in the sentence. This other verb may be written or understood. The past perfect action happens before the other past action in the sentence.*

When we **saw** his room empty, **we** all **knew** that **John had gone** to the movies.
**He had gone** before **we knew** it. **He had taken** his books with him.
After **he had finished** reading, **he went** to the movies.

B. *In each of the following sentences, use the past perfect tense of the verb in parentheses:*

1. He saw the skull. It _____ (be) _____ there a long time.
2. He wanted to tell about the skull that he _____ (find)
   _____.

3. The boss asked where he _____ (see) _____ the skull.
4. He said that it _____ (speak) _____ to him.
5. When they came to visit, we _____ (do) _____ our homework.
6. I bent to pick up my pencil, but it _____ (roll) _____ under the table.
7. Class _____ (begin) _____ before Mary came.
8. He said that it _____ (happen) _____ to him, too.
9. She _____ (start) _____ to wash the dishes when we called her.
10. He told the man he _____ (hear) _____ a voice.
11. The dog _____ (eat) _____ the chicken before he came out from under the table.
12. Before the dog spoke, the man _____ (stop) _____ running.
13. The boy _____ (stand) _____ on his head for five minutes when we saw him.
14. The boss didn't think that the skull _____ (speak) _____.
15. The girl _____ (pass) _____ the tree before she saw it.
16. The man saw that the boy _____ (ride) _____ his horse away.
17. The old man _____ (smoke) _____ a cigar before the doctor came.
18. When he _____ (pull) _____ up the weeds, he sat down.
19. The thief _____ (steal) _____ three sheep before the policeman caught him.
20. Before I bent down, she _____ (pick) _____ up the pieces of paper.

## II. WHAT AS SUBJECT OF NOUN CLAUSES

*From your reading:*

"Do you know **what I am going to do?**"
"I want to see for myself **what it says.**"

Structure (continued)

**A.** *A noun clause with <u>what</u> as the subject repeats a question, asked or understood.*

**What happened next?**
  Do you know **what happened next?**
  I don't know **what happened next.**
  Did they see **what happened next?**
  Yes, they saw **what happened next.**

**What am I going to do?**
  Will he guess **what I am going to do?**
  Yes, he will guess **what I am going to do.**
  Does she remember **what I am going to do?**
  No, she doesn't remember **what I am going to do.**

**B.** *In the past tense, this type of clause is used with the simple past form of the verb.*

**What did the girl want?**
  Do you know **what the girl wanted?**
  Yes, I know **what the girl wanted.**

**What did they see?**
  Will they tell us **what they saw?**
  No, they won't tell us **what they saw.**

**What did Sam want the skull to do?**
  Did the boss know **what Sam wanted the skull to do?**
  No, he didn't know **what Sam wanted the skull to do.**

**C.** *Practice forming the following questions into noun clauses:*
  *Examples: What is it? Do you know?*
    *Do you know **what it is?***
    *Yes, I know **what it is.** It's a window.*
  *What was the man looking at? Did you see?*
    *Did you see **what the man was looking at?***
    *Yes, I saw **what the man was looking at.** He was looking at a mule.*

1. What is the teacher's name? Does your friend know?
2. What did she want? Do you know?
3. What did he hear? Does he remember?
4. What is this? Do they know?
5. What did they want? Do you know?
6. What did he say? Did he forget?
7. What is my name? Do you know?
8. What is my address? Do you know?
9. What sound did we hear? Do you know?
10. What did he want to know? Do you remember?
11. What do cows eat? Do you all know?
12. What did Mary do? Does her mother know?
13. What did she do yesterday? Did you see?
14. What are you going to do tomorrow? Do you know?
15. What do children like to drink? Do mothers know?
16. What did that student say? Do you know?
17. What is your grandfather's name? Do you remember?
18. What does my father do? Do you know?
19. What is the longest day of the year? Do you remember?
20. What do mules eat? Do you know?

## Conversation

*Answer the following questions, using complete sentences:*

1. What did Sam talk about?
2. Where did he work?
3. What did he kick?
4. Where was he going when he kicked it?
5. Why did Sam become excited?
6. Who went with Sam to the woods?
7. Did the skull sing to Sam's boss?
8. What did the boss think about Sam?
9. Did the skull speak after the boss had gone away?
10. What was "the lesson"?
11. Do you think that Sam really had a *big* mouth? What do you think "a big mouth" means?

**Conversation** (continued)

12. When do we say "excuse me"?
13. What do you do when you drop your pencil?
14. Is there something in your pocket?
15. Which job do you prefer—washing dishes or cutting grass?
16. Is there anyone near the door?
17. Do you need your book any more?
18. Do you understand everything in this lesson?
19. Do you like to hear the sound of airplanes?
20. When do classes start here?

## Write or Tell

*A Job I Like*

*Something Sad*

## Dictation

*Listen to, repeat, and then write each of the following sentences:*

Sam was a man who couldn't stop talking. He talked about everything that he knew. He found a skull in the woods, but before he could pick it up, it spoke. Sam ran from the woods to tell what he had found. When he didn't hear a voice, his boss said, "I don't want you to work for me any more." Sadly Sam sat down on the ground beside his new friend.

# Pronunciation

| / iy / | / ɪ / | / ð / |
|--------|-------|-------|
| need | thick | there |
| tree | this | that |
| feet | kick | this |
| we | sit | those |
| please | bill | brother |
| | | the |

/ iy /     We don't need three feet.

/ ɪ /     This little kitten is sick.

/ iy, ɪ /     Please kick the little thing by the tree to me.

/ ð /     Those are the brothers there.

# Unit 10

# The Dream

Once there was an old man who had little gold, but he did have a big fat possum and a bag of sweet potatoes. He took the possum and the potatoes home and put them on the table. Then he got a few pieces of wood and some paper and made a fire. There was so much food he had to find two pans for it all. He put a large pan with the possum inside it on the fire and dropped the potatoes into another pan.

Then he sat down and waited for the possum and the potatoes to cook. The potatoes were soon done, but it took a long time for the possum. "I'll whistle while I wait," he said to himself. So he sat and whistled and watched the pan with the possum.

Finally, after a long while, the possum was cooked. The old

man took the pan with the possum off the fire and put it onto the table beside the sweet potatoes.

"There are few things I like more than hot possum," he said to himself, "but one thing I do like more than hot possum is cold possum. I'll let it cool a little while. I don't have to hurry." So he left the possum in the pan to cool, and he sat down in his chair again.

"I think I'll go to sleep," he said. "Then I'll dream about eating the possum. I'll enjoy eating it twice." So the old man sat back in his chair, closed his eyes, and fell asleep. He dreamed he was eating the possum, and his teeth went up and down.

A stranger who was passing the house smelled the possum. This stranger went quietly to the door and looked into the room. There he saw the pan on the table and the sleeping man. "I mustn't be noisy if I want to eat," thought the stranger. So he took the shoes off his big feet and went in. He lifted up the lid of the pan, and there was the possum. The sweet potatoes were on the table. There was a cooked possum and sweet potatoes and a hungry man. Now, do you know what happened?

Soon the possum was all bones, the potatoes were all peels, and the stranger was more than a man. He put the bones on one side of the table, and the potato peels on the other. He put a little possum gravy on the sleeping man's hands and mouth.

Then the stranger quietly left the house. A little while later the old man woke up. He opened his eyes, rubbed his stomach, looked at the pan, and laughed.

"Hello there, possum," he said. "You're in the pan, aren't you? I'll tell you hello now. Soon I must tell you good-bye!"

He went over to the pan and took off the lid, but he didn't see any possum.

"Where is my possum?"

He looked around for the potatoes, but he didn't see any potatoes.

"Where are my sweet potatoes?"

He found only some bones and a few potato peels. He sat down in his chair to think.

On his hands he saw some possum gravy. When he put out his tongue, he tasted possum gravy on his lips. He couldn't understand it.

Then he looked at his hands again. "The possum has been here," he said. He licked his lips. "The possum has been here, too." He rubbed his stomach. "But I don't think any possum has been here!"

## Vocabulary

| | | | |
|---|---|---|---|
| asleep | hand | peel | to taste |
| bone | hello | possum | tooth |
| cooked | to lick | quietly | tongue |
| to cool | lid | to rub | to wake |
| done | lip | shoe | while |
| to dream | must | to smell | to whistle |
| few | necessity | stomach | wood |
| gravy | pan | sweet | |

## Idioms

| | |
|---|---|
| to be cooked | to look around |
| to be done | to take a long time |
| to dream about (something) | to take (something) off |
| to fall asleep | to wake up |
| to go to sleep | |

## Related Words

| | | |
|---|---|---|
| cooked (adj.) | to peel (verb) | to taste (verb) |
| to cook (verb) | peel (noun) | taste (noun) |
| cook (noun) | peeling (noun) | tasty (adj.) |

to cool (verb)  
cool (adj.)

quietly (adv.)  
quiet (adj.)

to whistle (verb)  
whistle (noun)

to dream (verb)  
dream (noun)

to smell (verb)  
smell (noun)

## Opposites

cool—warm  
off—on  
quietly—noisily, loudly  
sweet—sour  
to take off—to put on  
to wake up—to go to sleep

## Structure

### I. LITTLE, FEW, A LITTLE, A FEW

*From your reading:*

There was an old man who had **little gold.**  
"There are **few things** I like more than hot possum."  
"I'll let it cool **a little while.**"  
He got **a few pieces** of wood.

**A.** *little = not much*  
*few = not many*

*a little = some*  
*a few = some*

*Little and a little are used with mass nouns:*

I have **little wood** to make a fire.  
There is **a little gravy** on his face.

*Few and a few are used with count nouns:*

There were **few strangers** around his farm.  
There are **a few spots** on his shirt.

**Structure** (continued)

> *B. Do this exercise first with the meaning <u>some</u>, then with the meaning <u>not much</u> or <u>not many</u>:*
>
>   1. I have _____ tickets to the ball game.
>   2. _____ people want to go outside when it rains.
>   3. I know _____ stories about dogs.
>   4. I know _____ people in this town.
>   5. He ate _____ of the cake.
>   6. There is _____ rice for you.
>   7. There are _____ pieces.
>   8. He has _____ ink.
>   9. I have _____ money.
>  10. There are _____ books here that I want to read.

## II. VERBS OF NECESSITY: <u>HAVE TO</u> AND <u>MUST</u> .

*From your reading:*

"Soon I **must tell** you good-bye."
"I **mustn't be** noisy if I want to eat."
There was so much food he **had to find** two pans.
"I don't **have to hurry**."

> *A. For the present, past, or future tenses, <u>have to</u> is used. <u>Must</u> has only a present tense form, though it is often used for future time.*
>
> He **has to study** English every day.
> He **had to study** English last year.
> He **will have to study** English next year.
> He **must study** English **every day**.
> Next year I **must buy** a new coat.

*In the affirmative form of the present tense, <u>must</u> and <u>have to</u> have the same meaning.*

must = have to
I **must take** my book home. = I **have to take** my book home.

*But in the negative form, <u>must</u> and <u>have to</u> have different meanings: If I <u>do not have to</u> do something, I myself can decide if I want to do it or not.*

The teacher says I **must not take** my book home.
( The teacher says to leave my books at school. )
The teacher says I **do not have to take** my book home.
( The teacher says I may take my book home if I want to, but I may leave it at school if I want to. )

PRESENT TENSE

| *Affirmative* | *Negative* |
|---|---|
| must | must not |
| have to, has to | do not have to, does not have to |
|  | don't have to, doesn't have to |

PAST TENSE

| *Affirmative* | *Negative* |
|---|---|
| had to | did not have to |
|  | didn't have to |

FUTURE TENSE

| *Affirmative* | *Negative* |
|---|---|
| will have to | will not have to |
| 'll have to | won't have to |
| must | mustn't |

**B. Use the most appropriate form in each of the following sentences:**

*Example: You _____ (negative) _____ walk on the grass.*
            *It is forbidden.*
            *You must not walk on the grass.*

1. I _____ [affirmative] _____ study English next year, because I am going to the University.
2. My brother _____ [affirmative] _____ study it last year, when he was in the United States.

**Structure (continued)**

3. You _____ [negative] _____ go with us, but you may if you like.
4. We _____ [negative] _____ ride the bus next year, but we may choose to.
5. He _____ [negative] _____ give her flowers, but he decided to.
6. We _____ [affirmative] _____ be home before six o'clock.
7. You _____ [negative] _____ forget your notebook. It is necessary for your work.
8. He _____ [affirmative] _____ wash his hands.
9. You _____ [negative] _____ walk so far. If you are ill, you must be careful.
10. His parents are very rich, so he _____ [negative] _____ work unless he wants to.

**C.** *Questions are usually made with* <u>have to</u> *instead of with* <u>must</u>.

**Do** you **have to go** home now?
**Don't** you **have to go** home now?
**Did** you **have to go** home then?
**Didn't** you **have to go** home then?
**Will** you **have to go** home after class?
**Won't** you **have to go** home after class?

**D.** *Form ten questions from the words in the following lists. Then answer the questions.*

*Example:* *Did she have to take care of the child last week?*
          *Yes, she had to take care of the child last week.*

| Verb | Subject | Verb phrase | Adverb |
|------|---------|-------------|--------|
| Do | I | wake up early | |
| Don't | you | close the door quietly | |
| Doesn't | he | lift the desk | now? |

| Verb | Subject | Verb phrase | Adverb |
|------|---------|-------------|--------|
| Did | she | get ready for school | tomorrow? |
| Didn't | we | get the book | last week? |
| Will | they | eat up the soup | |
| Won't | | come back to school | |
| | | take care of the child | |
| | | wash the dishes | |
| | | go to the office | |

## Conversation

*Answer the following questions, using complete sentences:*

1. Was the man who had the dream old or young?
2. What did he have in a bag?
3. With what did he make a fire?
4. Why didn't he eat the possum when he got home?
5. What did he do when he was waiting?
6. Who ate the possum?
7. Why didn't the man hear the stranger come in?
8. What did he dream about?
9. What did he taste on his mouth?
10. Where else was the gravy?
11. Is it easy to wake up in the morning?
12. Do you smell smoke now?
13. What are some things that we can cook in a pan?
14. Where are your teeth and tongue?
15. Are oranges sweet?
16. Is it easy to lift the teacher's desk?
17. Can you usually remember your dreams?
18. Is this classroom made of wood?
19. Can you whistle?
20. Do all animals have stomachs?

# Write or Tell

*An Interesting Dream*

*Something That Tastes Good*

# Dictation

*Listen to, repeat, and then write each of the following sentences:*

I must tell you a story about an old man. He had a possum and a few sweet potatoes. After he had cooked the food, he went to sleep and dreamed about it. A stranger stole the possum and ate everything except the bones. When the old man woke up, he licked his lips with his tongue and rubbed his stomach. But he found only peels and bones on the table, so he had to go to bed hungry.

# Pronunciation

| / ey / | / θ / | / ð / |
|--------|-------|-------|
| wait | think | there |
| stranger | teeth | another |
| table | mouth | this |
| taste | through | than |
| gravy | breath | breathe |

| | |
|--|--|
| / ey / | Wait for the stranger to taste the gravy. |
| / θ / | Three teeth are in his mouth. |
| / ð / | There is another brother. |
| / θ, ð / | Brother breathes through his teeth, I think. |

# Unit 11

# The Tar Baby

One day Rabbit said to himself, "It's too dry here. I need some water. I can drink dew in the mornings, but that isn't enough." So Brother Rabbit went to Brother Fox. He said, "Brother Fox, we all need water. Let's dig a well."

So Fox went and called all the other animals together. "Come. Let's dig a well for our water," he said. He got Brother Bear, Brother Possum, and Brother Coon.

When the animals had decided where to dig the well, they started to dig, and they asked Brother Rabbit to help them.

"I'm sick," said lazy Brother Rabbit.

"Come on," they said. "Help us dig this well. We all need water."

Rabbit said, "Oh, I don't need water. I can drink dew in the morning." So he didn't help. But when the other animals finished digging, he wanted some of the water. Of course, the other animals didn't let Rabbit take any water from the well, but he went at night and got a pan full of water.

The next day the angry animals saw Rabbit's footprints by the well.

"What can we do about Brother Rabbit?" they asked. "He thinks he is better than we are. He thinks he is the cleverest animal of all."

Bear said, "I'll tell you. I'll sit here by the well all night and catch him." So Bear sat by the well, but he went to sleep. Again Rabbit came and quietly stole some water.

"We must catch Brother Rabbit," the animals said the next day. "How can we do it?" Each animal spoke more excitedly than the one before. Brother Bear was the angriest of all, and he spoke the most loudly.

Then Brother Fox wanted to speak, and Brother Bear told the other animals to listen to him. "Brother Fox will know what to do," he said.

"I know how to catch him," said Brother Fox. "Let's make a tar baby and put it near the well. A tar baby is the best thing.

That night Brother Rabbit went to the well to get some water. He saw the tar baby and thought it was Brother Bear. "I can't get any water tonight," he thought. "There's Brother Bear waiting for me again." He looked a second time and said, "No, that isn't Bear. He's too little to be Brother Bear."

Rabbit went up to the tar baby and said, "Boo-oo-oo!"

The tar baby didn't move.

Then Rabbit put his face near the tar baby's face and said

again, "Boo!" The tar baby didn't speak. Rabbit ran around and around the tar baby and put his hand near the tar baby's face, but the tar baby stood still.

"I think that's only a piece of wood," Rabbit said, "or perhaps it's a sleeping man." Now he stood in front of the tar baby. "Hello, old man. What are you doing here?" he yelled.

The tar baby didn't answer.

"Don't you hear me?" asked Rabbit. "Speak, or I'll hit you." The tar baby said nothing, so Rabbit hit him. His hand stuck to the tar.

"Let me go. You were pretending that you were sleeping. Let me go, or I'll hit you with my other hand," yelled Rabbit angrily. Of course, the tar baby said nothing, so Rabbit hit him with his other hand. It stuck, too.

"Let me go, or I'll kick you," said Rabbit. The tar baby didn't say anything, so Rabbit kicked him and his foot stuck in the tar. Poor Rabbit! He didn't know when to stop. He kicked with his other foot, and it stuck, too.

The other animals were hiding in the grass, and when they saw Brother Rabbit stuck in the tar baby, they all ran out. "We've caught you," they said. "We are more clever than you. We've caught you, old Rabbit!"

"Oh, I'm so sick," said Rabbit.

"What shall we do with him?" asked one.

"Throw him into a fire," said another.

"Please, please throw me into a fire," said Rabbit. "I'm so cold."

"No, we can't do that," the other animals said. "He likes the fire."

One said, "Hang him," but another said, "He's too light to hang."

Finally they said to Brother Rabbit, "We're going to throw you into the water with a stone around your neck."

"Oh, yes," Rabbit said. "I love the water. Throw me in now. I want to visit my friend Brother Fish."

"We can't do that," the animals said. "Let's throw him into the brier patch."

"No, no," cried Rabbit, "please don't do that. The briers will tear my feet. They'll tear my skin. They'll tear my eyes out."

So the other animals picked Rabbit up and threw him into the brier patch. As Rabbit ran away through the briers, he yelled, "This is the nicest place I know of. This is my home. I was born in a brier patch!"

## Vocabulary

| | | | |
|---|---|---|---|
| anything | to describe | neck | tar |
| baby | dew | patch | to tear |
| bear | to dig | pattern | thorn |
| born | face | to pretend | until |
| brier | footprint | rabbit | well |
| brier patch | fox | skin | |
| clever | to hang | to stick | |
| comparison | irregular | stone | |
| coon | necessary | syllable | |

## Idioms

to be born

come on

to stick to (something)

What can we do about (something)?

What shall we do with (something)?

## Related Words

| | | |
|---|---|---|
| clever (adj.) | face (noun) | to stick (verb) |
| cleverly (adv.) | to face (verb) | sticky (adj.) |
| cleverness (noun) | | |
| | necessary (adj.) | to tear (verb) |
| comparison (noun) | necessity (noun) | tear (noun) |
| comparative (adj.) | | |
| to compare (verb) | | |

## Structure

### I. INFINITIVE PHRASES

*A. The verbs* <u>ask</u>, <u>want</u>, <u>tell</u>, *and* <u>let</u> *are often used with an infinitive phrase.*

*From your reading:*

They **asked** Brother Rabbit **to help** them.

"I **want to visit** my friend Brother Fish."

Brother Bear **told** the other animals **to listen** to Brother Fox.

The other animals **didn't let** him **take** any water from the well.

| Subject | Verb | Object of Verb | Infinitive | Object of Infinitive |
|---|---|---|---|---|
| She | asked | me | to sing | the song. |
| I | wanted | | to study | English. |
| John | told | them | to come. | |
| They | let | her | play. | |

*Make ten sentences using the pattern shown.*

**Structure (continued)**

REVIEW NOTE: *The verb let is used with the simple form of the verb.*

| She | **let** | the dog | **go.** |
|-----|---------|---------|---------|
| He | **lets** | us | **swim.** |

B. *An infinitive phrase is often used with how, what, when, and where.*

*From your reading:*

"I know **how to catch** him."
"Brother Fox will know **what to do.**"
He didn't know **when to stop.**
They had decided **where to dig** the well.

| Subject | Verb | Object of Verb | Connective | Infinitive | Object of Infinitive |
|---------|------|----------------|------------|------------|----------------------|
| He | knows | | when | to go. | |
| I | told | her | where | to study. | |
| She | asked | him | how | to sing | the song. |
| They | told | me | what | to do. | |

*Make ten sentences using the pattern shown.*

## II. COMPARISON OF ADJECTIVES

*From your reading:*

The **angry** animals saw Rabbit's footprints.
"We are **more clever than** you."
"This is **the best place that I know of.**"

A. *An adjective describes a person or thing.*
He is an **old man.**

*The comparative degree is used when two people or things are compared.*

John is **older than his brother.**

*The superlative degree is used when three or more people or things are compared.*

Our house is *the oldest house in town.*

Review Note: *We usually use the before the adjective in its superlative degree.*

B. *The comparative and superlative forms of one-syllable and some two-syllable adjectives are formed by the addition of er or est to the adjective.*

| old | older | (the) oldest |
| happy | happier | (the) happiest |
| long | longer | (the) longest |

*The comparative and superlative forms of many two-syllable adjectives, and of adjectives of three or more syllables, are formed by placing more or the most before the adjective.*

| beautiful | more beautiful | (the) most beautiful |
| careful | more careful | (the) most careful |

*Some adjectives have irregular comparisons.*

| bad | worse | (the) worst |
| far | farther | (the) farthest |
| good | better | (the) best |
| (a) little | less | (the) least |
| many | more | (the) most |
| much | more | (the) most |

*One may show comparisons of adjectives by placing less or the least before the adjective.*

This is not a comfortable desk.
It is **less comfortable than** your desk.
It is **the least comfortable desk of all.**

C. *Give the comparative or superlative degree of the adjective in each of the following sentences. Give each sentence first with the more or most (er or est) form of the adjective, and then with the less or least form.*

**Structure (continued)**

*Examples:* He was _____ (strong) _____ his friend.
He was **stronger than** his friend.
He was **less strong than** his friend.
He was _____ (strong) _____ boy in the class.
He was **the strongest** boy in the class.
He was **the least strong** boy in the class.

1. She is _____ (stingy) _____ old woman that I know.
2. This is _____ (quiet) _____ room in the school.
3. Apples are _____ (sweet) _____ oranges.
4. That is _____ (strange) _____ place I have seen.
5. _____ (Wild) _____ animals of all live in the woods.
6. He is _____ (strong) _____ person in this town.
7. He is _____ (thin) _____ I am.
8. It is _____ (good) _____ class in the school.
9. John is _____ (clever) _____ boy in class.
10. He is _____ (poor) _____ than his father was.
11. This is _____ (bad) _____ weather of the year.
12. Today the sky is _____ (dark) _____ yesterday.
13. New York is _____ (far) _____ away _____ London is.
14. She is _____ (smart) _____ he is.
15. The man is _____ (tall) _____ his son.
16. He is _____ (old) _____ his brother.
17. He is _____ (old) _____ person in his family.
18. That table is _____ (heavy) _____ my desk.
19. This is _____ (dirty) _____ book in the room.
20. This well is _____ (dry) _____ that one.

## III. COMPARISON OF ADVERBS

*From your reading:*

"Let me go," yelled Rabbit **angrily**.
Each animal spoke **more excitedly than the one before**.
Brother Bear spoke **the most loudly**.

**A.** *An adverb is used to describe an action.*

She **dances beautifully.**

*The comparative degree is used when two actions are compared.*

She dances **more beautifully than her sister does.**
She dances **more beautifully than she sings.**

*The superlative degree is used when three or more actions are compared.*

She dances **the most beautifully of all the dancers.**

**B.** *The comparative and superlative degrees of many adverbs are formed by placing* <u>more</u> *or* <u>the most</u> *before the adverb.*

   ·   quickly     more quickly    the most quickly

*A few adverbs are compared by adding* <u>er</u> *or* <u>est</u> *to the adverb.*

| | | |
|---|---|---|
| near | nearer | nearest |
| early | earlier | earliest |

*Some adverbs with irregular forms are*

| | | |
|---|---|---|
| badly | worse | worst |
| far | farther | farthest |
| much | more | most |
| little | less | least |
| well | better | best |

*Comparisons of adverbs may be shown with the use of the words* <u>less</u> *and the* <u>least</u>.

He didn't **do** his work **well.**
He did his work **less well than I did.**
He did his work **the least well of all of us.**

**C.** *Give the comparative degree of each of the following adverbs: first, using* <u>more</u>; *second, using* <u>less</u>.

**Structure** (continued)

> *Example: I came* ____ (*early*) ____ *the teacher.*
> *I came **earlier than** the teacher.*
> *I came **less early than** the teacher.*

1. Mary walks ____ (far) ____ I to school.
2. He speaks English ____ (well) ____ we.
3. I read ____ (slowly) ____ he.
4. He reads ____ (fast) ____ I.
5. He answered the questions ____ (quickly) ____ his older brother.
6. Now he speaks ____ (angrily) ____ when he came.
7. He speaks ____ (cleverly) ____ the others.
8. He slept ____ (uncomfortably) ____ his brothers.
9. The king walked ____ (proudly) ____ the servant.
10. The woman yelled ____ (excitedly) ____ her daughter.

*Read the above sentences again. This time use the superlative degree. Use* <u>of all</u> *instead of the second part of the comparison.*

> *Example: I came* ____ (*early*).
> *I came **the earliest of all**.*
> *I came **the least early of all**.*

# Conversation

*Answer the following questions, using complete sentences:*
1. Why did the animals need water?
2. Who said first, "Let's dig a well"?
3. Why didn't Brother Rabbit help dig the well?
4. What did Rabbit do at night?
5. Why didn't Brother Bear catch Rabbit?
6. How did the animals catch him?
7. Was Rabbit really sick?

8. Why didn't they throw him into a fire?
9. Did the briers tear Brother Rabbit's feet?
10. Who was the cleverest of the animals?
11. Where were you born?
12. Where can we find footprints?
13. What do we usually do with tar?
14. When is dew usually on the ground?
15. What is something that you can tear?
16. Have you ever seen a fox's footprints?
17. Have you ever drunk water from a well?
18. Do roses have thorns?
19. How many necks does a person have?
20. Are these desks very light?

## Write or Tell

*The Town Where I Was Born*

*An Animal Story*

## Dictation

*Listen to, repeat, and then write each of the following sentences:*

All the animals dug the well except Brother Rabbit. He stole his water at night, when Brother Bear was asleep. Brother Fox knew how to catch the thief. He told the others what to do. When Rabbit stuck to the tar baby, they all ran out of the tall grass and caught him. They threw him into the brier patch where he had been born, and he ran away.

# Pronunciation

| / ɛ / | / s / | / z / |
|-------|-------|-------|
| went | us | is |
| well | so | his |
| together | himself | themselves |
| yell | face | please |
| next | ask | was |
| said | answer | catches |
| when | excuse (noun) | excuse (verb) |

/ ɛ /   The next day, we said we went together to the well.

/ s /   He asked us himself what our excuse was.

/ z /   His home is in the briers.

/ s, z /   Please answer it yourselves.

# Unit 12

# Mrs. Simpson and Her Soup

One time Mrs. Simpson invited a lot of people to her house for dinner. She planned to feed them a good dinner of meat and vegetables and her special soup.

On the day of the party, everyone was busy at the Simpson house. Mrs. Simpson had five daughters, but no one thought about making the soup. They washed and ironed and cleaned the house. They made the dessert. Then Mrs. Simpson thought of the soup, and she ran to the kitchen to make it.

Adapted from B. A. Botkin, "Salting the Pudding."

Mrs. Simpson made the best soup in the town. No woman was a better cook than she was. But this time she forgot to put salt into it. Of course, a good soup needs some salt.

Mrs. Simpson made a bigger fire and put her soup on the stove. Then she began to sweep the floor. Her hands became very dirty.

Suddenly she thought about the soup. She had not put any salt into it! So she called one of her daughters to help her.

"Sue," she said, "will you put some salt into the soup? My hands are too dirty."

"I can't, Ma, I'm washing my hair," said Sue.

"Sara, will you go put salt into the soup?"

"I can't," said Sara. "Something is wrong with my dress and I have to sew it."

"Bertha, can you salt the soup?"

"No, Ma," said Bertha. "Ask somebody else to do it."

"Won't anyone help me? Jenny, go salt the soup."

"Tell Lil to do it, Ma. I'm ironing the tablecloth," Jenny said.

"I can't, Ma. I'm looking for my necklace. I'm not going to do anything else until I find it," Lil said.

So Mrs. Simpson put down her broom. She washed her hands and salted the soup. Then she began again to clean the floor.

Lil began to think that she should obey her mother, so she went quietly to the kitchen and salted the soup. After that she continued to look for her necklace. She looked into this corner and that.

Jenny began to be sorry that she had been rude, so she salted the soup, too. Then she finished the ironing.

Sue went into the kitchen and smelled the soup. "It will taste better with salt," she told herself, so she salted it.

Later Sara thought, "I really ought to help Ma," and she salted the soup. Then Bertha went quietly to the kitchen and salted the soup, too.

That night the hungry guests sat waiting for the soup. They could smell it, and it smelled good. Then Mrs. Simpson put it on the table in front of everyone. The preacher was there to dinner, so Mrs. Simpson gave him the first dish. He took a big mouthful of the soup. Suddenly his eyes opened wide. He picked up his glass of water and drank it all.

Now Mrs. Simpson knew that something was wrong, and she tasted the soup herself. Then she knew.

"Which one of you girls put salt into this soup?" she asked her daughters.

"I did, Ma," all five said together.

"And I did, too," Mrs. Simpson said. "Too many cooks spoil the broth."

And that's the truth.

## Vocabulary

| | | | |
|---|---|---|---|
| broom | to feed | preacher | to spoil |
| broth | guest | rude | to sweep |
| dish | necklace | salt | tablecloth |
| else | needle | to salt | thread |
| everyone | to obey | to sew | wrong |

## Idioms

something is wrong, something is wrong with (something)

## Related Words

| | | |
|---|---|---|
| to obey (verb) | salt (noun) | tablecloth (noun) |
| obedience (noun) | to salt (verb) | cloth (noun) |
| | salty (adj.) | table (noun) |
| rude (adj.) | | |
| rudely (adv.) | | to thread (verb) |
| rudeness (noun) | | thread (noun) |

# Opposites

to obey—to disobey
rude—polite

# Structure

## I. INDEFINITE PRONOUNS WITH <u>ANY</u>, <u>SOME</u>, <u>NO</u>, <u>EVERY</u>; USE OF <u>ELSE</u>

*From your reading:*

"Won't **anyone** help me?"

"Ask **somebody** else to do it."

**No one** thought about the soup.

**Everyone** was busy at the Simpson house.

### A. *Read these sentences:*

Will **someone** write on the board?

Yes, **someone** will write on the board.

Yes, **everyone** will write on the board.

No, **no one** will write on the board.

No, there **isn't anyone** who will write on the board.

Do you have **anything** in your desk?

Yes, I have **something** in my desk.

No, I don't have **anything** in my desk.

**Everything** is on my desk.

No, I have **nothing** in my desk.

### B. *Words formed from* <u>*any*</u> *are usually used in interrogative or negative sentences.*

Is **anybody** going to town after class?

No, there isn't **anybody** going to town.

*Words formed from* <u>*any*</u> *may be used in affirmative statements, such as the following:*

He is hungry. He will eat **anything** you give him.

**Anybody** can understand this sentence.

**C.** *Words formed from* <u>some</u> *are used in interrogative or affirmative sentences.*

Do you want **something** to read?
Yes, I want **something** from the library.

**D.** *A compound pronoun formed from* <u>no</u> *is negative, and there should be no other negative words used in the sentence in which it is used (except* <u>no</u> *at the beginning of an answer).*

Can anything help his cough?
No, **nothing can help** his cough.

Was anybody there?
No, **nobody was there.**

**E.** *All of these compound pronouns are singular in form.*

**Everybody wants** to dance.
**Nobody wants** to eat.
**Somebody is** coming.
**Is anybody** going?

**F.** <u>Else</u> *often follows one of these compound pronouns. It means* <u>other</u>.

I have a pen, but **no one else** has one.
Don't give the book to her. Give it to **someone else.**

**G.** *Use* <u>any</u>, <u>some</u>, <u>no</u> *or* <u>every</u> *to complete the compound pronoun in each of the following sentences:*

*Example: Is* _____ *body in class today? (all)*
        *Is everybody in class today?*

1. No, everybody is at home. There is _____*body* in class.
2. There isn't _____*one* here.
3. Is there _____*thing* more to eat? I'm still hungry.
4. No, there isn't _____*thing* else.
5. No, there is _____*thing* else.
6. _____*one* here can speak a little English. (all)
7. Did _____*one* have a wrong answer on the test?

**Structure** (continued)

8. No, _____*one* had the wrong answer on the test.
9. He doesn't want _____*body* to sit by him.
10. Does the teacher have _____*thing* in her hand?
11. No, she has_____*thing* in her hand.
12. _____*thing* that you need is on your desk. (all)
13. I know _____*thing* about horses, but not much.
14. Do you know _____*thing* about them?
15. He doesn't do _____*thing* except eat and sleep.
16. _____*one* salted the soup.
17. Does _____*body* else need a pencil?
18. No, _____*body* else needs one.
19. I don't think that _____*body* needs one.
20. Can you see _____*thing* on a dark night?

## II. VERBS OF NECESSITY: <u>SHOULD</u> AND <u>OUGHT TO</u>

*From your reading:*

Lil thought that she **should obey** her mother.
Sara thought, "I really **ought to help** Ma."

**A.** *The words <u>should</u> and <u>ought to</u> have the same meaning.*

should = ought to

**B.** *In the present tense, <u>should</u> and <u>ought to</u> are followed by the simple form of the main verb.*

I **should study** now.
I **ought to study** now.

| | |
|---|---|
| **Should** you **study** now? | **Ought** you **to study** now? |
| You **shouldn't study** now. | You **oughtn't to study** now. |
| **Shouldn't** you **study** now? | **Oughtn't** you **to study** now? |

**C.** *The past tenses of <u>should</u> and <u>ought to</u> are formed with the use of the present perfect tense.*

You **should have read** the lesson.
You **shouldn't have read** the lesson.
You **ought to have read** the lesson.
You **oughtn't to have read** the lesson.

**D. Answer the questions in this exercise with <u>should</u> or <u>ought to</u>. Use <u>yes</u> or <u>no</u> in your answer.**

*Example: Should the stranger take off his shoes?*
*        **Yes,** he **should** take off his shoes.*
*        **No,** he **shouldn't** take off his shoes.*

1. Oughtn't he to go to sleep?
2. Should he cook the possum in a pan?
3. Shouldn't he put the pan on the stove?
4. Should I read this story?
5. Ought you to write on the blackboard?
6. Oughtn't you to write a letter?
7. Should I turn off the light?
8. Ought that little girl to be here?
9. Shouldn't he wake up now?
10. Should the stranger walk quietly?

**E. Use the past form of <u>should</u> or <u>ought to</u> in each of the following sentences. First read all the sentences with the affirmative form; then read them all with the negative form:**

*Example: I ____ (wash) ____ the dishes. (should)*
*        I should have washed the dishes.*
*        I shouldn't have washed the dishes.*

1. You ____ (erase) ____ the blackboard. (ought to)
2. He ____ (eat) ____ the possum himself. (should)
3. She ____ (cook) ____ three chickens instead of two. (ought to)
4. It ____ (rain) ____ this morning. (should)
5. We ____ (go) ____ home at two o'clock. (ought to)
6. You ____ (taste) ____ the ice cream that we made last week. (ought to)
7. He ____ (smoke) ____ the cigar. (ought to)
8. They ____ (tell) ____ the truth. (should)
9. Mary ____ (put) ____ the gravy in a bowl. (ought to)
10. John ____ (see) ____ the stranger. (should)

# Conversation

*Answer the following questions, using complete sentences:*

1. How many daughters did Mrs. Simpson have?
2. What did she plan to give to the guests?
3. Who was busy?
4. Where did Mrs. Simpson put the soup?
5. What did she forget to put into it?
6. Whose hands were dirty?
7. Who was looking for her necklace?
8. What was Jenny doing?
9. Who got the first dish of soup?
10. Who spoiled the broth?
11. Does rice taste good without salt?
12. Should a child obey his parents?
13. Is it rude to say, "You are a good cook"?
14. What does one need to sweep the floor?
15. What does one need to sew?
16. Is everyone in class today?
17. Is an egg good when it has spoiled?
18. I broke my friend's pencil. What should I say?
19. I don't see my pen. What should I do?
20. You have a pencil and paper. Do you need anything else to write the exercise?

# Write or Tell

*The Best Day of the Week*

*A Polite Thing to Do*

# Dictation

*Listen to, repeat, and then write each of the following sentences:*

Mrs. Simpson invited a lot of people to dinner. She and her five daughters worked hard to get ready. Everyone forgot about Mrs. Simpson's special soup. Finally she thought about it herself and ran to make it, but she didn't put any salt into it. She told her daughters to salt the soup, but no one did. The girls should have obeyed their mother, but they didn't.

# Pronunciation

| / ey / | / ɛ / | / l / |
|--------|-------|-------|
| made | vegetable | smell |
| lady | very | salt |
| taste | best | until |
| later | said | look |
| gave | tell | mouthful |

| | |
|---|---|
| / ey / | The lady waited and made the soup later. |
| / ɛ / | "The best vegetables smell very good," she said. |
| / ey, ɛ / | She made the very best soup later. |
| / l / | We smelled the clean, salty water. |

# Unit 13

# Mr. Brown's Weakness

One night there was a big religious meeting in a field. Everyone was there—the mothers, the fathers, the children, the aunts, and the uncles. People came from all around to hear about good and bad. They listened and talked and sang all night.

There were four or five speakers there. When one became tired, another stood up and began to talk. They talked until early the next morning. Then everyone was sleepy and wanted to rest, so they all went home to sleep for a few hours.

The speakers went into a corn field to rest, too. They could have gone to sleep, but they didn't want to. Mr. Smith, Mr.

Jones, Mr. Black, Mr. White, and Mr. Brown sat in the field talking. They couldn't stop talking.

Mr. Smith said, "Brothers, all night we talked about sins and weaknesses. Think about it. There isn't a man with *no* weakness, is there? In fact, I have a weakness myself. I think I'll tell you about it. I love apples and grapes. When I see apples or grapes in somebody else's garden, I take a few."

They all listened to Mr. Smith's words. Then Mr. Jones asked, "Brothers, may I tell about my weakness, too?"

"Yes. Yes, you may," the others answered.

"I know it's all right to talk to you. You won't tell anyone else what I say. I like to eat a lot. I live with a man who sometimes kills a deer, and his wife cooks most of it for dinner. When we sit down for dinner, I could eat that meat all by myself. I love to eat more than anything else."

Then Mr. Black became impatient. He wanted to talk about himself. "Well, brothers, I have a bad weakness, too," he said. "I like to look at pretty young girls."

Mr. White said, "Brother, is it all right if I tell about my weakness now? I like to drink. I know you won't tell anyone else about this. Every time I see something strong to drink I want it."

The men talked until it was time for the meeting to begin again. Each of the speakers had told about his weakness except Mr. Brown. He just sat there. He listened quietly to the other men speak.

Then the men turned to Mr. Brown. "Do you have any weaknesses, brother?" they asked him. "We have been talking about our weaknesses since we came to this field, but you haven't said anything."

Mr. Brown spoke slowly. "Yes, I have a bad weakness too. But it's terrible. I can't tell you about it. You might be angry with me."

"It's all right," the others said. "We told about our bad weaknesses. You can tell about yours."

"I hate to tell you about it," said Mr. Brown. "I'm ashamed. But I might tell you."

"Please tell," they said.

"Well, all right," said Mr. Brown. "My weakness is gossip. I want to tell others about everything I hear. Now I may tell everyone at the meeting about your weaknesses. In fact, I can't wait to tell all the other people." And Mr. Brown hurried back to the place for the meeting.

It is good to know your own weaknesses, but don't tell them to a gossip!

## Vocabulary

| | | | |
|---|---|---|---|
| ashamed | to hate | permission | terrible |
| careful | impatient | possibility | weakness |
| to gossip | to kill | religious | well |
| gossip | may | request | |
| grape | might | sin | |

## Idioms

| | |
|---|---|
| all around | to make a request |
| to be ashamed | I can't wait to (do something); |
| every time | he couldn't wait to (do some- |
| in fact | thing) |
| to give permission | |

## Related Words

| | | |
|---|---|---|
| ashamed (adj.) | impatient (adj.) | religious (adj.) |
| to shame (verb) | impatience (noun) | religion (noun) |
| shame (noun) | impatiently (adv.) | |

careful (adj.)
care (noun)
carefully (adv.)

gossip (noun)
to gossip (verb)

to kill (verb)
killer (noun)

possibility (noun)
possible (adj.)
possibly (adv.)

sin (noun)
to sin (verb)
sinful (adj.)
sinner (noun)

weakness (noun)
weak (adj.)
weaken (verb)

## Opposites

careful—careless
to hate—to love
patient—impatient
weakness—strength

## Structure

### I. THE AUXILIARIES MAY, MIGHT, CAN, COULD

*From your reading:*

"I **may** tell everyone about your weaknesses."
"You **might** be angry with me."
"I **can't** wait to tell all the other people."
"I **could** eat that meat all by myself."

A. *The words may and can have the past-tense forms might and could, but the use of might or could does not always indicate past time. Sometimes they are used to refer to the present tense. May and might are usually used in the same ways. Both words show possibility: Perhaps the action of the main verb will happen.*

B. *Present or future time is shown by using may or might before the present-tense form of the main verb.*

He **may tell** the others now.
He **might talk** tomorrow.

Mr. Brown **may not tell** the others.
He **might not run** to them.

**Structure** (continued)

*Past time is formed by using may or might with the present perfect form of the main verb.*

> They **may have stayed** all night last night.
> He **might not have told** them yesterday.
>
> The woman **may not have gone** to the meeting.
> They **might not have taken** their lunch.

**C. Use may or might for each sentence in this exercise. First use the present or future time, and then use the past time.**

> (1) today.
> *Example: John _____ (sing) _____ in class*
> (2) yesterday.
>
> *John may sing in class today.*
> *John may have sung in class yesterday.*

1. They _____ (meet) _____ in the field
   (1) this afternoon.
   (2) last week.

2. She _____ (go) _____ home for lunch
   (1) today.
   (2) yesterday.

3. They _____ (sleep) _____ before the meeting
   (1) tonight.
   (2) yesterday.

4. The teacher _____ (write) _____ with the chalk
   (1) now.
   (2) in the last class period.

5. I _____ (want) _____ to see a movie
   (1) this evening.
   (2) when you did.

6. Brother Brown _____ (drink) _____ all the water
   (1) tonight.
   (2) last night.

(1) now.

7. Other people ____ (know) ____ about our weaknesses

(2) yesterday.

(1) tomorrow.

8. It ____ (not rain) ____

(2) on Friday.

(1) next week.

9. Mary ____ (send) ____ you a letter

(2) last week.

(1) today.

10. I ____ (not eat) ____ lunch with John

(2) one day
last month.

**D.** *The words* <u>may</u>, <u>can</u>, *and* <u>could</u> *are used to make requests or give permission.* <u>May</u> *is the polite form for making requests, but* <u>could</u> *is also used.*

**May I go** now?

Yes, you **may.**

**Could I come** again tomorrow?

Yes, you **could.**

"You **can't read** now," said his mother.

**Couldn't I come** again tomorrow?

You **may not play** with those boys.

**E.** *Give a short and a long answer to each of the following, using* <u>yes</u> *or* <u>no</u> *in the answers:*

*Example: May I see your book? (Yes)*

*Yes, you may.*

*Yes, you may see my book.*

1. Could I give it to you tomorrow? (Yes)
2. Can't you go with us to the movies? (No)
3. May John use your pencil? (Yes)
4. Could you tell me the answer to this question? (No)
5. Couldn't they speak less? (No)

**Structure** (continued)

6. May I see you before class tomorrow? (Yes)
7. Can't Mr. Smith visit the class? (No)
8. Can we talk about this story now? (Yes)
9. May I go home now? (Yes)
10. May Mary come in? (No)

## II. ADVERBIAL CLAUSES WITH <u>SINCE</u> AND <u>UNTIL</u>

*From your reading:*

"We have been talking **since we came to this field.**"
They talked **until the sun came up.**

**A.** *Read these sentences:*

We **won't** come inside **until it rains.**
We **didn't** come inside **until it rained.**
We **have been** inside **since it rained.**

**B.** *When the verb in the <u>until</u> clause is in the present tense, the verb in the main clause is in the future tense.*

We **will stay** outside **until it rains.**
We **will not come** inside **until it rains.**
We **won't come** inside **until it rains.**

*When the verb in the <u>until</u> clause is in the past tense, the verb of the main clause is also in the past tense.*

We **stayed** outside **until it rained.**
We **didn't come** inside **until it rained.**

**C.** *Usually the verb of a <u>since</u> clause is in the simple past tense, and the verb of the main clause is in the present perfect tense.*

We **have been** inside since it **began** to rain.

**D.** *Put the verbs in the following sentences into the right tense:*

*Example: Until the teacher comes the students ___ (sit) ___ at their desks.*

*Until the teacher comes the students will sit at their desks.*

1. We _____ (not go) _____ home until the bell rings.
2. Since Mr. Smith ran away, they _____ (be) _____ unhappy.
3. Until my friend came, I _____ (wait) _____ in the classroom.
4. I _____ (not eat) _____ grapes since I ate some bad ones in September.
5. He _____ (not be) _____ angry until his friend gossiped.
6. Until his boss came, he _____ (speak) _____ with the skull.
7. Since the old man went to sleep, he _____ (dream) _____ of the possum.
8. They _____ (sit) _____ by a tree until the others returned.
9. She _____ (forget) _____ to salt the soup since she put it on the stove.
10. She _____ (not salt) _____ it until her daughter comes.

## Conversation

*Answer the following questions, using complete sentences:*

1. Where did the people have their meeting?
2. What did they do at the meeting?
3. Did the speakers sleep? Why or why not?
4. What did the men talk about when they were together?
5. What was Mr. Jones's weakness?
6. How long did the men talk together?
7. Did Mr. Brown have a weakness?
8. Did he tell about himself?
9. What did Mr. Brown do after he told about his weakness?

**Conversation (continued)**

10. Should you tell a gossip about your weaknesses?
11. Men say that women like to gossip. Do you think this is true?
12. Are you careful when you are on the street?
13. Do we sometimes have terrible weather here?
14. Do you hate to listen to gossip?
15. Can you name several religions?
16. Which has more strength, a rabbit or a dog?
17. Do grapes grow in your country?
18. Are mothers usually patient with their children?
19. Are policemen patient or impatient with careless drivers?
20. Do you usually tell your thoughts to your friends?

# Write or Tell

*A Bad Weakness*

*A Time to Be Careful*

# Dictation

*Listen to, repeat, and then write each of the following sentences:*

Most people say that they have a weakness or two. Some of us are too impatient, and some of us like to gossip. Some are careless, and others have bad thoughts. Mr. Brown wanted to tell about others' weaknesses. He couldn't wait to tell other people. The speakers didn't love him when he gossiped, because they were ashamed of their weaknesses.

# Pronunciation

| / uw / | / m / |
|--------|-------|
| you    | time  |
| too    | mouth |

| / uw / | / m / |
|--------|-------|
| coon | morning |
| rude | meat |
| broom | animal |
| tooth | meeting |

/ uw /  You saw the coon's tooth, too.

/ m /  The time animals eat meat is morning.

# Unit 14

# She Is His

One time there was a farmer's daughter that no man wanted to marry. The daughter worked hard and made good pie and cake, but she had a sharp tongue. She was always fussing. Her old father used to think unhappily, "She'll be with me always!"

But one day a strong young man with a beard came to the farm and asked the girl to marry him. She said, "Yes," and they went straight to the preacher. After they were married, they started toward the husband's house.

---

Adapted from Richard Chase, "That's Once."

The man had a sick old mule that was almost dead. He rode on this mule, and his wife rode behind him. They had a big bag full of their belongings on the mule behind them both.

Soon they passed a beautiful farm. "Do you see this farm and the beautiful house?" the man asked.

"Yes," she said.

He rubbed his beard. "Well, these are mine," he said.

The old mule went along until it was tired. Then it fell, and the man and his wife fell beside it. The woman didn't say anything. The man pulled the mule to its feet and said to it, "That's once!"

They got on the mule again. Soon they passed a field full of fat sheep. One was fatter than all the others. The woman was looking at it when her husband spoke. "Do you see all these sheep?" he asked.

"Yes," she said.

He rubbed his beard. "Well, these are mine," he said.

A mile down the road the mule fell again, and of course the man and wife fell, too. The man pulled the mule to its feet and said, "That's twice!"

They got on the mule again and rode along. They passed a field full of fat pigs.

"Do you see these pigs?" he asked.

"Yes."

He rubbed his beard. "Well, these are mine," he said.

After a time the mule fell again. This time the wife fell on her head, but she didn't complain. She was so quiet that her husband thought she was sick. The man looked at the poor mule and said, "That's three times!" and he took his gun and shot the old animal dead.

The woman was surprised. She opened her mouth, but she didn't say a thing. She picked up their belongings, and they continued along the road. After a long walk they came to a dirty little house. The windows were broken and there were some thin pigs. A few were sitting in the doorway, but the hungrier ones were trying to find something to eat.

Then the woman lost her temper. "Why did we come *here?*" she asked. "Isn't the farm that we saw yours? Aren't those beautiful fields yours?"

"Why, no," said her husband. "I said the hairs of my beard are mine."

"Why did you bring me to this dirty place?" she yelled. "You do one foolish thing after another. You lied to me. You shot the mule, and this bag is so heavy that I'm almost dead. You are a fool. I'm not going to stay here with you. Do you think I like this place? I used to live in a good home. Do you think I like your silly beard?"

The man looked his wife in the eye and said, "That's once!"

After that, she closed her mouth and never opened it again, except to eat.

## Vocabulary

| | | | |
|---|---|---|---|
| beard | to complain | to fuss | sharp |
| beautiful | dead | habitual | sill, |
| behind | dirt | mile | temper |
| belongings | doorway | pig | |
| both | fool | probably | |
| broken | foolish | result | |

## Idioms

| | |
|---|---|
| to go along | to shoot (someone, something) |
| to lose one's temper | dead |
| to ride along | used to (do something) |
| a sharp tongue | to work hard |

## Related Words

beautiful (adj.)
beautifully (adv.)
beauty (noun)

belongings (noun)
to belong (verb)

broken (adj.)
to break (verb)

dead (adj.)
the dead (noun)
death (noun)

dirty (adj.)
dirt (noun)

foolish (adj.)
fool (noun)
foolishly (adv.)
to fool (verb)

habitual (adj.)
habit (noun)

probably (adv.)
probable (adj.)

sharp (adj.)
to sharpen (verb)

## Opposites

beautiful—ugly
behind—ahead, ahead of
dead—alive
foolish—wise
heavy—light
to lose one's temper—to keep one's head
sharp—dull

## Structure

### I. ADVERBIAL CLAUSES WITH <u>SO</u> . . . <u>THAT</u>

*From your reading:*

She was **so quiet that** her husband thought she was sick.
"This bag is **so heavy that** I'm almost dead."

**Structure** (continued)

### A. Read the following sentences, noticing the word order:

| Subject | Verb of Being | so | Adjective | that | Adverbial clause of result |
|---|---|---|---|---|---|
| 1. She | was | so | happy | that | she sang a song. |
| 2. The bag | was | so | light | that | she could carry it. |
| 3. I | am | so | tired | that | I want to go home. |
| 4. The boys | are | so | full | that | they don't want cake. |
| 5. He | is | so | silly | that | he laughs at me. |

| Subject | Action Verb | so | Adverb | that | Adverbial clause of result |
|---|---|---|---|---|---|
| 1. The old man | ran | so | fast | that | he became tired. |
| 2. The woman | spoke | so | sharply | that | no one liked her. |
| 3. She | complained | so | much | that | her father didn't want her. |
| 4. We | work | so | hard | that | we don't have time to play. |
| 5. Mules | move | so | slowly | that | I don't like to ride them. |

### B. Complete the following sentences. Some take adjectives and some take adverbs:

Example: *I sometimes am_____I have to go to bed.*
*I sometimes am so sleepy that I have to go to bed.*

1. The pencil was _____ I didn't need to sharpen it again.
2. The mule was _____ it couldn't walk.
3. My sister is _____ she never makes a mistake.
4. The boys were _____ they wanted to drink lots of water.
5. The story was _____ I couldn't sleep all night.
6. The house was _____ she wanted to go away.

7. They are _____ they are always finished early.
8. The sun was _____ we didn't need coats.
9. My brother went to bed _____ he slept until ten this morning.
10. He spoke _____ we didn't hear him.
11. The boy drove his car _____ he almost hit some people.
12. The people outside yelled _____ we couldn't hear you.
13. He ate the soup _____ he never finished it.
14. He sings _____ I always like to listen to him.
15. He is usually patient, but this time he spoke _____ I was surprised.

## II. THE INDEFINITE PRONOUNS ONE AND THE OTHER

*From your reading:*

**One** was fatter than all **the others**.

**A few** were sitting, but **the hungrier ones** were looking for food.

**A.** *Some pronouns are called indefinite pronouns because they do not refer to definite persons or things. One and the other are indefinite pronouns.*

*When both* one *and* the other *are used in a sentence,* one *usually precedes* the other.

The books are here. **One** is red, and **the other** is blue.
Both girls are pretty, but **one** is prettier than **the other**.

*When* the other *is used and* one *is not, a noun or another pronoun usually precedes* the other.

**This book** is heavy. **The other** is light.
**He** is a quiet boy, but **the other** is noisy.
I know **the smaller girl,** but I don't know **the other**.

**Structure** (continued)

> <u>One and the other</u> have plural forms, <u>the ones and the others</u>.

> **The pencils in the box** are newer than **the others**.
> **The ones** on the table are old.
> **He** is going, but **the others** aren't.

**B. Complete the following sentences with the singular or plural forms of <u>one</u> or <u>the other</u>:**

1. She has two sons; _____ is tall, and _____ is short.
2. _____ is taller than _____.
3. The two boys are foolish, but _____ is more foolish than _____.
4. Both books are interesting, but _____ is more interesting than _____.
5. There were many dresses in the store. She liked the red dress, but she didn't like _____.
6. She thought the black _____ were not very beautiful.
7. These are the _____ I like; I think the _____ are ugly.
8. This pencil is sharp but _____ is dull.
9. The _____ in your hand is sharp, too.
10. Both students are good, but _____ is better than _____.
11. _____ of those two houses is bigger than _____.
12. There are two baskets of eggs. The eggs in this basket are brown, and _____ are white.
13. When there are two people together, _____ is usually taller than _____.
14. Is _____ of your hands stronger than _____?
15. These pieces of chalk are white. Are _____ white, too?

## III. THE SIMPLE PRESENT TENSE AND <u>USED TO</u> FOR HABITUAL ACTION

*From your reading:*

"I **used to live** in a good home."

Her father **used to think** she would never marry.

### A. *Present*

She **makes** good pies.

**Does** she **make** good pies?

    Yes, she **does.**

    Yes, she **makes** good pies.

*Past*

She **used to make** good pies. (She made good pies in the past. Perhaps she doesn't now.)

**Did** she **use to make** good pies?

    Yes, she did.

    Yes, she **used to make** good pies.

### B. *From each of the following sentences form a question about habitual action and give a long answer, first in the present time and then in the past with* <u>*used to*</u>:

*Example: We begin our class at eight o'clock.*

                *Do we begin our class at eight o'clock?*

                *Yes, we begin our class at eight o'clock.*

                *Did we use to begin our class at eight o'clock?*

                *Yes, we used to begin our class at eight o'clock.*

1. He **has** a beard.
2. She **lives** with her father.
3. The pigs **sit** on the steps.
4. The sheep **are** fat.
5. The woman **loses** her temper easily.
6. The old man **wakes** up at six o'clock.
7. The rabbit **lives** in the brier patch.
8. His wife **likes** to gossip.
9. I **catch** fish in the river.

**Structure** (continued)

10. She **complains** about the hard work that she does.
11. The boys **play** in the woods.
12. His mother **milks** the cows.
13. The children **pretend** to be cowboys.
14. She **cries** when she reads a sad story.
15. He **sits** on his porch every evening.

# Conversation

*Answer the following questions, using complete sentences:*

1. Did the daughter like to work hard?
2. What was she always doing?
3. Was her husband young and strong?
4. Was the mule young and strong?
5. What did they see in the fields?
6. What did they have in the bag?
7. Did the woman complain on the trip?
8. Did the man shoot his wife?
9. When did the woman lose her temper?
10. Do you think the man was foolish?
11. Is it usually wise to keep one's temper?
12. Do you have many belongings in the classroom?
13. Is someone in the doorway?
14. Does a pig eat more than a sheep?
15. Can you see some dirt on the floor?
16. Is there a beautiful tree near the window?
17. Is the teacher behind his desk?
18. Are your books very heavy?
19. Shall we continue this lesson tomorrow?
20. Is it probably going to rain tomorrow?

## Write or Tell

*A Wise Person I Know*

*A Beautiful Thing*

## Dictation

*Listen to, repeat, and then write each of the following sentences:*

An old farmer used to think that no man wanted to marry his daughter. Then she married a young man with a beard and rode along home with him. They passed a farm and two fields. In one field were pigs and in the other were sheep. The woman thought that the beautiful fields and the farm were his. When the old mule fell down three times, her husband shot it. "That's three times," he said. When his wife complained, he said "That's once!" She closed her mouth so that he might not lose his temper.

## Pronunciation

| / ʊ / | / n / |
|-------|-------|
| foot | no |
| look | one |
| woman | man |
| pull | went |
| book | mine |

/ ʊ / The woman looked at the book.

/ n / No one knew when the man went.

# Unit 15

# The Race

*"Old Man" was the most important god of many American In-*
*dians. In some Indian stories he is strong and kind; in others he is*
*weak and mean. What is he in this story?*

❖ ❖ ❖

Once Old Man was walking along when he heard some very
strange singing. He looked all around to see who it was. Finally
he saw some cottontail rabbits, singing and making magic. They
had made a fire which had a lot of ashes. They lay down in the
ashes and sang while one rabbit covered the others up. The sing-

128

ing rabbits could stay under the ashes only a short time because they were very hot.

"Little Brothers," said Old Man, "that is amazing magic. You lie in those hot ashes and don't burn. Please teach me how to do it."

"Come on then, Old Man," said the rabbits, "and we will show you. You must sing our song and stay in the ashes only a short time." Old Man began to sing, and he lay down. The rabbits covered him with hot ashes that did not burn him because he stayed in them only a few minutes.

"That is very nice," he said. "Now I understand your magic as well as you do. Lie down and let me cover you up."

The rabbits all lay down in the ashes, and Old Man covered them up. He put so many hot ashes over them that they could not leave the fire, and they began to burn. Only one frightened rabbit got away. Old Man wanted to put her into the ashes again.

"Please don't put me into the ashes," she cried. "My small children are alone. I must go and take care of them."

"All right," said Old Man. "You may go, but I will cook the others."

He put some more wood on the ashes. When the rabbits were as hot as the fire, he took them out.

While Old Man waited for the rabbits to cool, he sat down. A coyote came along, limping very badly.

"Old Man," said the coyote, "you have a lot of cooked rabbits. Give me one of them."

"Go away," said Old Man. "You're lazy. Catch your own rabbits."

"My foot is broken," said the coyote. "I can't catch anything, and I'm very hungry. Give me only half a rabbit."

"These are my rabbits," said Old Man. "I won't give you any. But I'll race you to that hill. If you get to the hill first, you may have a rabbit."

"All right," said the coyote. They started. Old Man ran very fast, but the coyote limped along. When they were near the hill, suddenly the limping coyote turned around and stopped limping. He then ran back very fast, because his foot was not broken at all. It took Old Man a long time to go back. As he got to the fire, the coyote ate the last rabbit and ran away.

## Vocabulary

| | | | |
|---|---|---|---|
| amazing | to cover | kind | to race |
| as | coyote | lazy | while |
| ash | exactly | to limp | |
| to burn | god | magic | |
| cottontail rabbit | hill | race | |

## Idioms

| | |
|---|---|
| to cover (something) up | to go back |
| to get to (somewhere) | to lie down |
| go away | not at all |

## Related Words

| | | |
|---|---|---|
| amazing (adj.) | hill (noun) | magic (noun) |
| to amaze (verb) | hilly (adj.) | magic (adj.) |
| amazed (adj.) | | magical (adj.) |
| amazement (noun) | lazy (adj.) | magically (adv.) |
| | lazily (adv.) | magician (noun) |
| to burn (verb) | laziness (noun) | |
| burn (noun) | | race (noun) |
| | to limp (verb) | to race (verb) |
| to cover (verb) | limp (noun) | racer (noun) |
| cover (noun) | | |

# Opposites

to cover—to uncover
lazy—hard-working
to lie down—to get up

# Structure

## I. ADVERBIAL CLAUSES WITH <u>AS</u> AND <u>WHILE</u>

*From your reading:*

They sang while one rabbit covered the others.
As he got to the fire, the coyote ran away.

**A.** *As and <u>while</u> are used to connect two actions that happen at exactly the same time. They are used at the beginning of the sentence or between the two clauses.*

Old Man ran ahead as the coyote limped slowly along.
As the coyote limped slowly along, Old Man ran ahead.
As Old Man ran ahead, the coyote limped slowly along.
The coyote limped slowly along as Old Man ran ahead.
While Old Man waited for the rabbits to cool, he sat down.
Old Man sat down while he waited for the rabbits to cool.

**B.** *Connect the following clauses, using <u>as</u> or <u>while</u>:*

1. The boy yelled _____ he ran away.
2. We waited for her _____ she went shopping.
3. He threw stones at the bear _____ the others yelled.
4. He slept _____ the others worked.
5. _____ we lay in the sun, we heard a strange noise.
6. _____ she ironed the clothes, her sister cleaned the room.
7. Rabbit laughed _____ the other animals became more angry.

**Structure** (continued)

8. _____ her son looked at the cow, the mother held the rope.
9. The old man sat in a chair _____ he slept.
10. The stranger went quietly away _____ the old man slept.

## II. PRESENT AND PAST PARTICIPLES AS ADJECTIVES

*From your reading:*

one *frightened* rabbit
the *singing* rabbits
the *limping* coyote

### A. *Compare the following:*

John is an interesting boy. (I think John is interesting. He interests me.)

That is a frightening man. (I think the man is frightening. He frightens me.)

John is an interested student. (John himself is interested in his studies.)

That is a frightened man. (The man himself is afraid; he is frightened. Someone or something frightens him.)

### B. *In these sentences, use the present or past participle as indicated in the parentheses:*

*Example: The _____ (shake) _____ boy stood in the dark room. (present)*

*The shaking boy stood in the dark room.*

1. The mother picked up her _____ (cry) _____ baby. (present)
2. He didn't say the _____ (expect) _____ word. (past)
3. The little girl put her _____ (pull) _____ tooth on the table. (past)
4. We saw the _____ (climb) _____ men from the bottom of the hill. (present)

5. The _____ (smoke) _____ cigarettes are in the ash tray. (past)
6. My _____ (finish) _____ exercise is on the desk. (past)
7. The window is closed, so we can't hear the _____ (yell) _____ boys. (present)
8. Old Man heard the _'__ (sing) _____ rabbits. (present)
9. I spoke to the _____ (worry) _____ mother. (past)
10. The _____ (move) _____ hand writes. (present)

## III. COMPARISON OF ADJECTIVES AND ADVERBS WITH AS . . . AS AND NOT SO . . . AS

*From your reading:*

I understand your magic as well as you do.
The rabbits were as hot as the fire.

A. **With as . . . as, people or things or actions that are the same in some way are compared.**

The girl is as big as her mother.
She is as clever as her sister.
She speaks English as well as I do.

B. *Negative comparisons are made with not so . . . as. Also, in conversation, negative comparisons are often made with not as . . . as.*

I am not so afraid as you.
Matthew is not so interested as John.

C. *Use as . . . as and not so . . . as to compare each of the following: first, in the affirmative; second, in the negative.*
*Example: Our class is _____ (quiet) _____ the other.*
        *Our class is as quiet as the other.*
        *Our class is not so quiet as the other.*

1. This board is _____ (dirty) _____ the other.
2. The first girl is _____ (stingy) _____ the second.

**Structure ( continued )**

3. This dishcloth is _____ ( dry ) _____ that one.
4. My pencil is _____ ( sharp ) _____ yours.
5. Some stories are _____ ( true ) _____ life.
6. Now he is _____ ( deaf ) _____ he was last year.
7. That old man was _____ ( mean ) _____ his neighbor.
8. His back is _____ ( straight ) _____ mine.
9. The fox is _____ ( wild ) _____ the bear.
10. John is _____ ( strong ) _____ his friend.
11. She is _____ ( thin ) _____ she was last year.
12. Today is _____ ( cool ) _____ yesterday.
13. He is _____ ( careful ) _____ his brother.
14. She is _____ ( tall ) _____ her sister.
15. Their team is _____ ( good ) _____ our team.
16. Today she is _____ ( impatient ) _____ she was yester-day.
17. This piece of paper is _____ ( dry ) _____ yours.
18. My shoes are _____ ( black ) _____ the others.
19. It is seven o'clock in the evening. It is ___( light )___ day.
20. A rabbit is _____ ( clever ) _____ a fox.

# Conversation

*Answer the following questions, using complete sentences:*

1. What were the rabbits doing when Old Man first saw them?
2. What did he call the rabbits?
3. Did Old Man lie down in the ashes?
4. What did he do to the rabbits?
5. Did any of the rabbits get out of the fire?
6. What did Old Man do while he waited for the rabbits to cool?
7. Did Old Man believe that the coyote's foot was broken? Why?
8. Why did they run to the hill?
9. Which one ran the faster?

10. Which one ate the rabbits?
11. Do you know any magic tricks?
12. Does a person limp when he burns his hand?
13. Is this school on a hill?
14. Where do you usually sit while you study?
15. Do you know any strange stories?
16. Do you prefer cooked or raw vegetables?
17. What falls from a cigarette as it burns?
18. Does a lazy student learn much?
19. Are the people in this room familiar to you?
20. In this weather do people need covers on their beds at night?

## Write or Tell

*Something Amazing*

*A Race I Have Seen*

## Dictation

*Listen to, repeat, and then write each of the following sentences:*

As Old Man was traveling, he saw some cottontail rabbits lying in a fire. The singing rabbits taught him how to lie down in the hot ashes, too. But Old Man was not so nice as the rabbits and he cooked them. While he was waiting for them to cool, a limping coyote asked him for one to eat. Old Man didn't get anything at all, because he was not so fast as the coyote.

## Pronunciation

| / uw / | / ʊ / | / r / |
|--------|-------|-------|
| you    | look  | strange |
| do     | could | rabbit |

**Pronunciation** (continued)

| / uw / | / ʊ / | / r / |
|--------|-------|-------|
| to | put | short |
| soon | took | strong |
| cool | foot | run |
| who | | near |

| | |
|---|---|
| / uw / | Whom do you want to see so soon? |
| / ʊ / | He could look at the foot. |
| / uw, ʊ / | Who could soon put the coon out to cool? |
| / r / | The stranger is near the short strong rabbit. |

# Appendixes

# TABLE OF
# PUNCTUATION MARKS

| | |
|---|---|
| Period | . |
| Comma | , |
| Semicolon | ; |
| Colon | : |
| Parentheses | ( ) |
| Quotation marks | " " |
| Question mark | ? |
| Apostrophe | ' |
| Dash | — |
| Exclamation point | ! |

# GUIDE TO PRONUNCIATION

## Vowel Sounds

| | |
|---|---|
| / ɪ / | sister |
| / ɛ / | set |
| / æ / | sat |
| / ɑ / | scar |
| / ɔ / | saw |
| / o / | so |
| / ʊ / | stood |
| / ə / | sudden |
| / ɚ / | sir, turn |

## Diphthongs

| | |
|---|---|
| / iy / | see |
| / ey / | say |
| / ɑɪ / | high |
| / ɑʊ / | how |
| / ɔɪ / | boy |
| / ow / | go |
| / uw / | moon |

## Consonant Sounds

| | |
|---|---|
| / b / | book |
| / d / | dark |
| / f / | fall |
| / g / | gold |
| / h / | hand |
| / k / | kind |
| / l / | land |
| / m / | milk |
| / n / | nose |
| / p / | pan |
| / r / | rabbit |
| / s / | sad |
| / t / | tooth |
| / v / | voice |
| / w / | wild |
| / y / | yard |
| / z / | freeze |
| / hw / | where |
| / ŋ / | sing |
| / θ / | thin |
| / ð / | then |
| / ʃ / | she |
| / tʃ / | chimney |
| / ʒ / | pleasure |
| / dʒ / | judge |

# GLOSSARY OF
# GRAMMATICAL TERMS

**Adjective**   An adjective describes a noun or pronoun:
*big* cat, *red* door, *happy* day

Descriptive adjectives have three forms ( see **Comparison** ).
Some adjectives do not take different forms.
*My, your, his* ( possessive adjectives )
*A, an, the* ( articles )
*This, that, all* ( indicator words )

**Adverb**   An adverb may work as follows:

To modify a verb: He ran *quickly.*
To modify an adjective: She is *very* pretty.
To modify another adverb: She speaks *too* slowly.
To modify a sentence: *Perhaps* they will come.

There are many different kinds of adverbs:
Adverbs of assertion: *No,* I will *not* go.
Adverbs of frequency: *always, ever, never, often, sometimes,
usually.*
Adverbs of manner: She sang *sweetly.*
Adverbs of measure: He sees *little.*
Adverbs of place: We went *inside.*
Adverbs of time: I'll see you *tomorrow.*

Relative adverbs:
*As* a father, he is kind; *as* a teacher, he is not.
She came *before* I did.

I have not seen him *since* last month.
They will stay *until* next Monday.
I will go *when* he goes.
I go *where* I am told.
She will rest *while* he works.

**Article** See **Adjective.**

**Auxiliary verb** An auxiliary verb helps another verb. Usually it is not used alone, except in answer to a question:

*Will* he come tomorrow? Yes, he *will.*
You *should* go home now.

**Clause** A clause is a group of words that includes at least a subject and a verb.
See **Dependent clause** and **Independent clause**

**Comparison** Adjectives and adverbs have three degrees of comparison:

| | *Adjective* | *Adverb* |
|---|---|---|
| Positive | He is a *tall* man. | She sings *sweetly.* |
| Comparative | He is *taller* than his brother. | She sings *more sweetly* than I. |
| Superlative | He is the *tallest* man in this room. | She sings the *most sweetly* of all of us. |

**Conjunction** A conjunction connects words, phrases, or clauses:

Simple conjunctions: *and, but, or*
Relative adverbs: *where, before, while*
Relative pronouns: *who, whose, which, what*

**Degree** See **Comparison.**

**Dependent clause** A dependent clause is part of a sentence. It has at least a subject and a verb but is not a complete sentence by itself.

Clauses are named according to the way they are used in the sentence:

Adjective clause: The boy *who knew the lesson* wrote on the blackboard.

Adverbial clause:
Of cause: He was late *because his clock broke.*
Of comparison: She was not as happy *as the boy was.*
Of condition: *If you go,* I will go.
Of place: We shall go *where we want to go.*
Of purpose: We came *so that we might learn.*
Of result: It was late, *so we went home.*
Of time: We'll go *when the bell rings.*

Noun clause: She said *that we must read the book.*

**Direct object**   The action of the verb in a sentence is performed upon a direct object:

I write *letters.*
He kicked *the ball.*

**Frequency words**   See **Adverb.**

**Future tense**   See **Verb.**

**Gerund**   A gerund is formed by adding *ing* to the simple form of the verb. A gerund is used as a noun.

I like *singing,* but I don't like *reading.*

**Independent clause**   An independent clause has a verb and a subject, and may stand alone as a sentence:
He studies English.

It may be combined with another independent clause:
He studies English, but *he wants to go to France.*

It may be combined with a dependent clause or phrase:
He studies English *without a teacher.*

**Indefinite pronoun**   See **Pronoun.**

**Indirect object**   The action of the verb in a sentence may be done *to* or *for* some indirect object. The indirect object directly follows the verb:
He gave *me* his book.

A prepositional phrase (preposition + object) may be used instead of an indirect object. A prepositional phrase does not need to follow the verb.
He gave the book *to me.*

**Infinitive**   An infinitive is the simple form of a verb. It usually follows *to.* It may be used as the object of the main verb in a sentence:
She wants *to read* now.

It may be used without *to* with certain verbs:
I can *swim.*

**Main verb**   See **Verb** and **Phrase.**

**Noun**   A noun is a word used to name a person or thing. Mass nouns (or "noncountable" nouns) name things that are usually not counted:
*water, happiness, cattle*

Count nouns name things that can be counted:
*book, chair, boy*

Count nouns may be singular or plural in number:
Singular: Nouns are singular when they name one person or thing: a *man,* that *house,* one *piece*

Plural: Nouns are plural when they name more than one person or thing: all the *men,* two *houses,* both *pieces*

**Number** "Number" refers to the form of a word: singular or plural. In English, nouns, pronouns, and verbs show number by their form. In a sentence, the subject and verb must agree in number:

One *man goes* home.
Two or more *men go* home.

**Object** See **Direct object, Indirect object, Preposition,** and **Pronoun.**

**Participle** The present and past participles are the forms of verbs used for the progressive tenses and the perfect tenses. See also **Verb.**

A participle may be used as an adjective:
Present participle: That is an *interesting* story.
Past participle: I am an *interested* student.

**Past participle** See **Participle.**

**Past perfect tense** See **Verb.**

**Past progressive tense** See **Verb.**

**Past tense** See **Verb.**

**Perfect tense** See **Verb.**

**Person** Pronouns have different forms not only for singular and plural number, but for *person.* "First person" is the person speaking, "second person" is the person who is being spoken to, and "third person" is the person who is being spoken of. See also **Pronoun.**

**Phrase** A phrase is a group of related words.

Types of phrases are:

Adjectival: A soup *of meat and vegetables* is nice.

Adverbial: *In the evening* we went to the movie.

Gerund: *Making shoes* is hard work.

Infinitive: *To change one's habits* is not easy.

Noun: *The little girl's mother* is sick.

Participial: The dog is unhappy *tied to the tree.*

Prepositional: *Behind the house* is a tree.

**Plural**   See **Noun** and **Pronoun.**

**Possessive**   See **Pronoun.**

**Preposition**   A preposition connects a noun (or a word or group of words used as a noun) with some other part of a sentence. Some common prepositions are:

*against, at, beside, by, far from, in, near, on, over, under, up, with.*

The noun that follows the preposition is called the object of the preposition:

The book is on the *table.*

He went to *town* yesterday.

**Present participle**   See **Participle.**

**Present perfect tense**   See **Verb.**

**Present tense**   See **Verb.**

**Progressive tense**   See **Verb.**

**Pronoun**   A pronoun is a word used instead of a noun:

John gave some flowers to Sally.

*He* gave *them* to *her.*

*Who* is at the door?

*I* am at the door.

Personal pronouns:

FIRST PERSON

|            | Singular  | Plural    |
|------------|-----------|-----------|
| Subjective | I         | we        |
| Objective  | me        | us        |
| Possessive | my, mine  | our, ours |
| Reflexive  | myself    | ourselves |

SECOND PERSON

|            | Singular     | Plural       |
|------------|--------------|--------------|
| Subjective | you          | you          |
| Objective  | you          | you          |
| Possessive | your, yours  | your, yours  |
| Reflexive  | yourself     | yourselves   |

THIRD PERSON

|            | Singular                   | Plural         |
|------------|----------------------------|----------------|
| Subjective | he, she, it                | they           |
| Objective  | him, her, it               | them           |
| Possessive | his, her, hers, its        | their, theirs  |
| Reflexive  | himself, herself, itself   | themselves     |

Indefinite pronouns: *some, any, each, every, anybody, everybody, nobody, somebody.*

Interrogative pronouns: An interrogative pronoun is the subject of a question:
*Who* is coming to see you?
*Which* of the books did you read first?
*What* is that little boy doing?

Relative pronouns: A relative pronoun introduces a dependent clause:
I don't see the boy *who bit me.*
People *whose dogs are noisy* are noisy, too.
The book *that he was reading* had colored pictures.
She knows *which foods he likes.*
That is the girl *whom I saw in a tree.*

**Relative**  See **Adverb, Conjunction,** and **Pronoun.**

**Sentence**  A sentence contains at least one independent clause, which may be connected to other clauses, dependent or independent. It has at least one subject and one verb and gives a complete thought: *She is my friend.*

**Simple present tense**  See **Verb.**

**Singular**  See **Noun, Number,** and **Pronoun.**

**Subject**  The subject of a verb may be a noun or noun substitute (pronoun). The subject performs the action given by the verb: *John* gave her some flowers.

**Tense**  See **Verb.**

**Verb**  A verb names an action or a state of being.

Action: He *kicks* the ball.
State of being: I *am* happy.

The main verb is the action word in a clause with more than one verb:

He had better *wear* his coat.
You should *see* this book.

An auxiliary verb helps the main verb:
You *should* learn your lesson.

Tenses:

| SIMPLE PRESENT | PRESENT PROGRESSIVE | PRESENT PERFECT |
|---|---|---|
| I write | I am writing | I have written |
| PAST | PAST PROGRESSIVE | PAST PERFECT |
| I wrote | I was writing | I had written |
| FUTURE | FUTURE PROGRESSIVE | FUTURE PERFECT |
| I will write | I will be writing | I will have written |
| I shall write | I shall be writing | I shall have written |
| I am to write | I am going to be writing | |

# VOCABULARY

Numbers refer to units. Numbers in boldface type—for example, **3, 8**—indicate that the word is discussed in the text of that particular unit. Words with which the student is probably already familiar are not followed by unit numbers.

Word forms are presented as follows:

Verbs are presented in infinitive, present participle, simple past, and past participle forms. If the simple past tense and the past participle are spelled the same, the last form presented is both simple past tense and past participle.

Nouns are presented in singular and plural forms. If the plural form is spelled simply by adding *-s* or *-es,* the noun is spelled out only once. For example, **boss, -es** indicates that the plural of *boss* is spelled exactly like the singular, with the addition of *-es: bosses.*

Adjectives and adverbs are presented in positive, comparative, and superlative degrees. If the comparative and superlative degrees are formed with *more* and *most,* the adjective or adverb is spelled out only once. For example, **afraid, more —, most —** indicates that the comparative degree of *afraid* is *more afraid,* and the superlative degree is *most afraid.*

**a, an**
**about**
   to dream about, 10
   to tell about, 8

to think about, 7
to worry about, 6
What can we do about (something)? 11

become, becoming, became, be-
    come, 5
bed, -s
    to go to bed
bedroom, -s
before
begin, beginning, began, be-
    gun, 5
behind, 14
belief, -s, 7
believable, more —, most —, 7
believe, believing, believed, 7
belong, belonging, belonged,
    14
belongings, 14
bend, bending, bent, 6
beside, 4
best
better
big, bigger, biggest
bird, -s
bit, -s, 9
    a little bit, 9
black
blind, 5
blue
boat, -s
    by boat
bone, -s, 10
book, -s
born, 11
    to be born, 11
boss, -es, 9
both, 14
bottom, -s, 8
box, -es

boy, -s
branch, -es, 3
break, breaking, broke, broken,
    14
breakfast, -s
    eat breakfast
    get breakfast
    have breakfast
breath, -s, 2
breathe, breathing, breathed, 2
brier, -s, 11
    brier patch, 11
bright, -er, -est
broken, 14
broom, -s, 12
broth, 12
brother, -s
brown
burn, -s, 15
burn, burning, burned, 15
bus, -es
    by bus
business, -es
busy, busier, busiest
but
    not only . . . but also
butter
buy, buying, bought
by
    by boat
    by oneself, 3
    by the table
    to come by, 4

cake, -s
    a piece of cake

call, calling, called
can, could, 13
 What can we do about (something)? 11
 What can we do with (something)? 11
 I can't wait to (do something), 13
captain, 8
car, -s
 by car
care
 take care of (something), 5
careful, more —, most —, 13
carefully, more —, most —, 13
careless, 13
carry, carrying, carried
cat, -s
catch, catching, caught, 3
ceiling, -s
cemetery, cemeteries, 7
cent, -s
chair, -s
chalk
 a piece of chalk
 pieces of chalk
change, changing, changed, 1
 to change one's mind, 1
cheap, -er, -est
cherry, cherries
chicken, -s, 1
 a piece of chicken
 pieces of chicken
child, children
chimney, -s, 3
choice, -s, 8

choose, choosing, chose, chosen, 8
chorus, -es
church, -es
cigar, -s, 7
cigarette, -s, 7
city, cities
class, -es
 to come to class
 to go to class
classroom, -s
clause, -s
clean, -er, -est, 3
clean, cleaning, cleaned
clear, -er, -est, 7
clever, -er, -est, 11
cleverly, more —, most —,
climb, climbing, climbed, 3
climber, -s, 3
clock, -s
close, closing, closed
cloth, -s, 12
clothes
coat, -s
coffee
 a cup of coffee
 cups of coffee
cold, -er, -est
college, -s
 to go to college
color, -s
comb, -s, 1
comb, combing, combed, 1
come, coming, came, come
 to come along, 7
 to come by, 4

Come on.
to come up to (something)
  It's good of you to come, 5
comfort, -s, 8
comfortable, more —, most —,
  8
comparative, 11
compare, comparing, com-
  pared, 11
comparison, -s, 11
complain, complaining, complained, 14
complete, completing, completed, 1
compliment, -s, 1
composition, -s
Congress, 1
congressman, congressmen, 1
conjunction, -s
connect, connecting, con-
  nected, 1
continue, continuing, continued, 6
contraction, 5
conversation, -s
cook, -s, 10
cook, cooking, cooked, 10
cooked, 10
  to be cooked, 10
cool, -er, -est, 10
cool, cooling, cooled, 10
coon, -s, 11
  raccoon, 1
corn, 5
  an ear of corn, 7
corner, -s

correct
cottontail rabbit, -s, 15
could, 13
  as fast as he could, 7
country, countries
course
  of course
cousin, -s
cover, -s, 8
cover, covering, covered, 15
  to cover (something) up, 15
cow, -s, 3
coyote, -s, 15
crazily, more —, most —, 4
craziness, 4
crazy, crazier, craziest, 4
crooked, more —, most —, 6
cross, crossing, crossed
cup, -s
cure, -s, 7
  to be cured, 7
cut, cutting, cut

dance, dancing, danced
dark, -er, -est, 7
  too dark to see, 7
darkness, 7
date, -s
daughter, -s
day, -s
  day or night, 7
dead, 2
  to shoot dead, 2
deaf, 5
deafness, 5
death, -s, 2, 14

December
decide, deciding, decided
  to decide to (do something)
degree
describe, describing, described, 11
desk, -s
dessert, -s
devil
  the Devil, 7
dew, 11
dictation
die, dying, died, 2
different, 8
dig, digging, dug, 11
dining room, -s
dinner, -s
  eat dinner
  get dinner
  have dinner
direct object, -s
dirt, 14
dirty, dirtier, dirtiest, 3
disappear, disappearing, disappeared, 5
disappearance, -s, 5
discomfort, -s, 8
dish, -es, 12
dishonest, more —, most —, 8
disobey, disobeying, disobeyed, 12
divide, dividing, divided, 7
do, doing, did, done, 2
  do the shopping
  How do you do?
  What do you do?

What can we do about (something)? 11
What can we do with (something)? 11
doctor, -s
dog, -s
dollar, -s
done
  to be done, 10
door, -s
doorway, -s, 14
down, 3
  down the road, 8
  to fall down, 4
  to lie down, 15
  to put (something) down, 7
  to sit down, 2
downstairs
downtown
dream, -s, 10
dream, dreaming, dreamed, 10
  to dream about (something), 10
dress, -es
dress, dressing, dressed
  to be dressed
  to get dressed
drink, drinking, drank, drunk
drive, driving, drove, driven
driver, -s
drop, dropping, dropped, 2
dry, drier, driest, 3
dry, drying, dried, 3
dryness, 3

each
early, earlier, earliest

ear, -s, 4
  an ear of corn, 7
  ears of corn
earth
  at the end of the earth, 1
  to the ends of the earth, 1
east
easy, easier, easiest
eat, eating, ate, eaten
  to eat breakfast, lunch, or dinner
education
egg, -s
eight
eighth
either, 2
eleven
eleventh
else, 12
emphasis, 3
empty, 1
empty, emptying, emptied, 1
emptiness, 1
end, -s
  at the end of the earth, 1
  to the ends of the earth, 1
end, ending, ended
enemy, enemies, 1
English
enjoy, enjoying, enjoyed
enough, 8
envelope, -s
erase, erasing, erased
eraser, -s
evening, -s
  Good evening.
  in the evening

ever, 7
every
  every day
  every Sunday
  every time, 13
everybody, 7, 12
everyone, 12
everything, 9, 12
exactly, 15
example, -s
except
excite, exciting, excited, 7
excited, more —, most —,
excitement, 7
exciting, more —, most —, 7
excuse, -s, 9
excuse, excusing, excused, 9
  Excuse me, 9
exercise, -s
expect, expecting, expected, 5
expectation, -s, 5
expensive, more —, most —
explain, explaining, explained
eye, -s, 2
  to look (someone) in the eye, 2
eye glasses, 6

face, -s, 11
face, facing, faced, 11
fact, -s
  in fact, 13
fall, -s, 4
fall, falling, fell, fallen, 4
  to fall asleep, 10
  to fall down, 4
  to fall off, 6

false
familiar, more —, most —, 5
family, families
famous, more —, most —
far, farther, farthest
   far away, 4
   far from (somewhere), 4
farm, -s
farmer, -s
fast, -er, -est, 7
   as fast as he could, 7
fat, fatter, fattest, 7
father, -s
favorite
feather, -s, 1
February
feed, feeding, fed, 12
feet, see foot
few, -er, -est, 10
   a few, 10
field, -s
fifteen
fifteenth
fifth
fill, filling, filled
final, 1
finally, 1
fine, finer, finest
   I'm fine, thank you.
finger, -s, 4
finish, finishing, finished, 6
fire, -s
first
   at first
fish
fisherman, fishermen, 4

fishing
   to go fishing
five
floor, -s
flower, -s
folk, 1
follow, following, followed, 1
following, 1
food
   some food
fool, -s, 14
fool, fooling, fooled, 14
foolish, more —, most —, 14
foolishly, more —, most —, 14
foot, feet, 2
   from head to foot, 4
footprint, -s, 11
for
   for a week
   for breakfast
   to get ready for (something), 5
   to look for (something), 1
   to wait for (something), 4
form, -s, 9
form, forming, formed, 9
found
four
fourteen
fourteenth
fourth
fox, -es, 11
Friday
friend, -s
friendly, friendlier, friendliest, 1

**from**
   away from (something), 4
   to come from (somewhere)
   far from (somewhere), 4
**from . . . to . . .**
   from head to foot, 4
   from morning to night
   from my house to your house
**front, -s**
   in front of (something), 7
**frown, -s, 5**
**frown, frowning, frowned, 5**
**fruit**
   a plate of fruit
**full, -er, -est, 1, 8**
**funny, funnier, funniest**
**further, furthest**
**fuss, fussing, fussed, 14**


**game, -s**
**garden, -s**
**generally**
**generous, more —, most —**
**get, getting, got, gotten**
   to get breakfast, lunch, dinner
   to get dressed
   to get home
   to get into (something), 4
   to get old, 6
   to get out of (something), 4
   to get ready for (something), 5
   to get (something) ready, 1
   to get (somewhere), 15
   to get up, 2, 4, 15

**girl, -s**
**give, giving, gave, given**
   to give permission, 13
**glad, gladder, gladdest, 4**
   I'm glad to meet you.
**glass, -es**
**glasses, 6**
   a pair of glasses
**go, going, went, gone**
   to go along, 14
   go away, 15
   to go away, 1
   to go back, 15
   to go to bed
   to go to class
   to go fishing
   to be gone, 1
   to go to school
   to go shopping
   to go to sleep, 10
   to let go of (something), 4
**god, -s, 15**
**gold, 3**
**good, better, best**
   good afternoon
   good-bye
   good evening
   good morning
   good night
   It's good of you to come, 5
   to pay good money for, 8
**gossip, 13**
**gossip, gossiping, gossiped, 13**
**government, -s**
**grab, -s, 4**
**grab, grabbing, grabbed, 4**

graduate, graduating,
    graduated
grape, -s, 13
grass
gravy, 10
gray
green
ground, 7
guest, -s, 12
gun, -s, 1

habit, -s, 14
habitual, 14
hair, -s, 1
   a lot of hair
half, halves
   half past ten
hand, -s, 10
hang, hanging, hanged, hung,
   11
happen, happening, happened,
   9
happening, -s, 9
happily, 1
happiness, 1
happy, happier, happiest, 1
hard, -er, -est
   to work hard, 14
hard-working, more —, most
   —, 15
hat, -s
hate, hating, hated, 13
have, having, had
   to have breakfast, lunch,
     dinner

to have to (do something), **10**
to have the right to (do
   something), 8
to have time, 1
he
head, -s, 1
   from head to foot, 4
hear, hearing, heard
heart, -s, 8
heavily, 6
heaviness, 6
heavy, heavier, heaviest, 6
hello, 10
help
   to give help
help, helping, helped
her
herself, 3
here
hero, heroes, 1
hide, hiding, hid, hidden, 1
high, -er, -est
hill, -s, 15
hilly, 15
him
himself, 3
his
history, histories
hold, holding, held, 3
home, -s
honest, more —, most —, 8
honesty, 8
horse, -s, 3
hot, hotter, hottest
hour, -s
house, -s

**housewife, housewives**
**housework**
   a lot of housework
**how**
   How are you?
   How do you do?
   how long
   how many
   how much
   how often, 1
   How old are you?
**hundred**
   a hundred
   one hundred
   three hundred
**hungry, hungrier, hungriest**
**hurry**
   in a hurry
**hurry, hurrying, hurried**
**husband, -s**

**I**
**ice**
   a lot of ice
**idiom, -s**
**if**
**impatience, 13**
**impatient, more —, most —, 13**
**impatiently, more —, most —,**
   13
**impolite, more —, most —, 1**
**important, more —, most —**
**in**
   in back of (something), 7
   in fact, 13
   in front of (something), 7

   in a hurry
   in the morning
**Indian, -s**
**indoors**
**infinitive, -s**
**ink**
**instead, 1**
   instead of (something), 1
**interesting, more —, most —**
**interrogative**
**into**
   to get into (something), 4
**introduce, introducing,**
    **introduced**
**invitation, -s**
**invite, inviting, invited**
**iron, -s**
**iron, ironing, ironed**
**irregular, 11**
**is**
**it**
**itself, 3**

**January**
**job, -s, 9**
**July**
**jump, jumping, jumped**
**June**
**just, 5**

**keep, keeping, kept**
   to keep (doing something), 6
   to keep on (doing some-
    thing)
   to keep one's temper, 14
**kick, kicking, kicked**

kill, killing, killed, 13
killer, -s, 13
kind, -er, -est, 15
kitchen, -s
knife, knives
know, knew, known

lake, -s
lamp, -s
language, -s
large, larger, largest
last
  last week
late, later, latest
laugh, laughing, laughed
lazily, more —, most —, 15
laziness, 15
lazy, lazier, laziest, 15
leaf, leaves
learn, learning, learned
leave, leaving, left, 5
  to leave (someone) alone, 5
less, 9
lesson, -s
let, letting, let
  to let go of (something), 4
letter, -s
library, libraries
lick, licking, licked, 10
lid, -s, 10
lie, -s, 2
  to tell a lie, 2
lie, lying, lied, 2
lie, lying, lay, lain
  to lie down, 15

lift, lifting, lifted, 2
light, -s
light, -er, -est, 6, 7
like, 1
  to be like (something else), 1
like, liking, liked
  to like to (do something)
limp, 15
limp, limping, limped, 15
lip, -s, 10
list, -s, 8
listen, listening, listened
  to listen to (something)
little, littler, littlest
  little, **10**
  a little, **10**
  a little bit, 9
live, living, lived
  to live alone, 3
living room, -s
loneliness, 3
lonely, lonelier, loneliest, 3
long, -er, -est
  to take a long time, 10
look, looking, looked
  to look around, 10
  to look for (something), 1
  to look (someone) in the eye,
    2
  to look at (something), 4
lord
  the Lord, 6
lose, losing, lost, 1
  to lose one's temper, 14
lot, -s
  a lot of

love, 6
  much love
love, loving, loved, 6
lucky, luckier, luckiest
  to be lucky
lunch

machine, -s
magic, 15
magical, 15
magically, 15
magician, -s, 15
make, making, made
  to make (someone) angry, 8
  to make a cake
  to make a mistake, 8
  to make a request, 13
  to make a sound, 9
man, men
manner, 8
many, more, most
  How many?
March
market, -s, 8
married
  to be married
marry, marrying, married
match, -es, 1
  shooting match, 1
May
may, might, 13
me
  Excuse me, 9
meal, -s
mean, -er, -est, 5
mean, meaning, meant

meaning, -s
meanness, 5
meat
  a piece of meat
meet, meeting, met
might, 13
mile, -s, 14
milk
  a glass of milk
milk, milking, milked, 3
million, -s
  a million people
  millions of people
mind, 1
  to change one's mind, 1
mine
minute, -s
  ten minutes to three
Miss
mistake, -s, 8
  to make a mistake, 8
mock, mocking, mocked, 4
mockery, 4
modern, more —, most —
modify, modifying, modified, 8
Monday
money
  much money
  to pay good money for
    (something), 8
month, -s
more
morning, -s
  Good morning.
  in the morning
  yesterday morning

most
mother, -s
mouth, -s, 4
move, moving, moved
movie, -s
Mr.
Mrs.
much, more, most
mud, 4
muddy, muddier, muddiest, 4
mule, -s, 2
music
must, 10
my
myself, 3

name, -s
near, -er, -est
necessary, more —, most —, 11
necessity, necessities, 10
neck, -s, 11
necklace, -s, 12
need, needing, needed
needle, -s, 12
negative, 2
neighbor, -s, 6
never, 7
new, -er, -est
newspaper, -s
next
  next month
  next to (something)
nice, nicer, nicest
night, -s
  at night
  day or night, 7

Good night.
  last night
nine
ninth
no
nobody, 7, **12**
noise, -s
  to make a noise
noisily, more —, most —, 10
noisy, noisier, noisiest
noncountable noun
noon, -s
no one, **12**
north
not
  not at all, 15
  not only . . . but also . . . .
  not so . . . as, **15**
notebook, -s
nothing, 9, **12**
noun, -s
November
now
number, -s
nurse, -s

obedience, 12
obey, obeying, obeyed, 12
object, -s
o'clock
  It's ten o'clock.
**October**
of
  to be afraid of (something), 2
  ahead of, 14
  in back of (something), 7

of course
in front of (something), 7
to get out of (something), 4
It's good of you to come, 5
instead of (something), 1
to let go of (something), 4
out of (something), 8
the rest of (something), 3
to take care of (something), 5
to be tired of (something), 3
**off**
to fall off, 6
to shoot (something) off, 1
to take (something) off, 10
**often, -er, -est, 7**
how often, 1
**old, -er, -est**
to get old, 6
How old are you?
**on**
come on, 11
to keep on (doing something), 3
to put (something) on, 10
on Sunday
on time
**once**
once upon a time, 2
**one, 14**
**oneself, 3**
**only**
**onto, 8**
**open, opening, opened**
**opposite, -s, 1**
**or**
day or night, 7

**oral**
**orally**
**order, 8**
**other, -s, 14**
**ought, 12**
**our**
**ourselves, 3**
**ours**
**out**
to get out of (something), 4
out of (something), 8
**outdoors**
**outside**
**over**
**owe, owing, owed**
**own**
my own book
**own, owning, owned**

**page, -s**
**pair, -s**
**pan, -s, 10**
**pants, 4**
a pair of pants
**paper, -s**
a lot of paper
a lot of test papers
**parent, -s**
**part, -s**
**pass, passing, passed, 3**
**pat, patting, patted, 1**
**patch, -es, 11**
**patient, more —, most —, 13**
**pattern, -s, 11**
**paw, -s, 1**
**pay, paying, paid**

to pay for (something)
to pay good money for (something), 8
peel, -s, 10
peel, peeling, peeled, 10
pen, -s
pencil, -s
people
perhaps
period, -s
permission, 13
   to give permission, 13
person, -s
phrase, -s
pick, picking, picked, 3
   to pick up, 7
picture, -s
piece, -s
   a piece of paper
pig, -s, 14
pipe, -s, 5
pitcher, -s, 1
place, -s
   to take place, 6
   adverb of place, 8
plan, -s
plan, planning, planned
plate, -s
play, playing, played
   to play football
   to play the piano
please
P. M.
point, pointing, pointed
   to point (something) at
      (something), 1

to point to (something), 1
policeman, policemen
polite, more —, most —, 1
politeness, 1
politely, more —, most —, 1
popular, more —, most —
porch, -es, 5
possibility, possibilities, 13
possible
possum, -s, 10
potato, -es
   sweet potatoes, 10
pound, -s, 8
pour, pouring, poured
practice, practicing, practiced
preacher, -s, 12
precede, preceding, preceded, 8
prefer, preferring, preferred
prepare, preparing, prepared
preposition, -s
president, -s
pretend, pretending, pretended,
   11
pretty, prettier, prettiest
price, -s
pride, 6
probable, more —, most —, 14
probably, more —, most —, 14
pronoun, -s
pronounce, pronouncing,
      pronounced
pronunciation
proud, -er, -est, 6
proudly, more —, most —, 6
pull, pulling, pulled, 4
punctuation mark, -s

punish, punishing, punished, 8
punishment, -s, 8
push, -es, 4
push, pushing, pushed, 4
put, putting, put
    to put (something) down, 7
    to put (something) on, 10
    to put (something) up, 1

question, -s
quick, -er, -est, 2
quickly, more —, most —, 2
quiet, -er, -est, 10
quietly, more —, most —, 10

rabbit, -s, 11
raccoon, 1
    coon, 11
race, -s
race, racing, raced, 15
rain
    much rain
rain, raining, rained
read, reading, read
ready
    to be ready
    to get (something) ready, 1
    to get ready for (something), 5
reason, -s
receive, receiving, received, 1
red
related, 1
religion, -s, 13
religious, more —, most —, 13
remember, remembering,

    remembered, 1
rent, renting, rented
repeat, repeating, repeated
repetition, -s
request, -s, 13
    to make a request, 13
rest, 3
    the rest of (something), 3
rest, resting, rested
result, -s
reward, rewarding, rewarded, 8
rheumatism, 7
ride, -s, 6
ride, riding, rode, ridden, 6
    to ride along, 14
rider, -s, 6
right
    to have the right to (do something), 8
river, -s, 1
road, -s
    down the road, 8
roll, -s, 8
roll, rolling, rolled, 9
room, -s
rope, -s, 2
rub, rubbing, rubbed, 10
rude, ruder, rudest, 1, 12
rudely, more —, most —, 12
rudeness, 12
run, running, ran, run
    to run away, 3

sad, sadder, saddest, 1, 9

sadly, more —, most —, 9
sadness, 9
salt, 12
salt, salting, salted, 12
salty, saltier, saltiest, 12
Saturday
save, saving, saved, 6
say, saying, said
scales, 8
school, -s
  go to school
  at school
  in school
season, -s
seat, -s
second
see, seeing, saw, seen
  too dark to see, 7
seem, seeming, seemed
seldom, 7
sell, selling, sold
send, sending, sent, 1
sentence, -s
September
serious, more —, most —
servant, -s, 3
seven
seventh
several
sew, sewing, sewed, sewn, 12
shake, shaking, shook, shaken,
  2
shall, 5
sharp, -er, -est, 14
  a sharp tongue, 14
sharpen, sharpening,

sharpened, 14
she
sheep, sheep, 7
shirt, -s, 4
shoe, -s, 10
shoot, shooting, shot, 1
  to shoot at (something), 1
  shooting match, 1
shop, -s
shop, shopping, shopped
  to go shopping
short, -er, -est
shot, 1
should, 12
show, showing, showed,
  shown
sick, -er, -est, 7
sickly, 7
sickness, -es, 7
side, -s, 8
silly, sillier, silliest, 14
silver, 3
  pieces of silver
simple, simpler, simplest, 2
sin, -s, 13
sin, sinning, sinned, 13
since, 13
sing, singing, sang, sung
single
sister, -s
sit, sitting, sat
  to sit down, 2
  to sit up, 5
six
sixth
size, -s

skin, -s, 11
skull, -s, 9
sleep, sleeping, slept
    to go to sleep, 10
sleepy, sleepier, sleepiest
    to be sleepy
slip, slipping, slipped, 4
slippery, more —, most —, 4
slow, -er, -est, 2, 7
slowly, more —, most —, 2
small, -er, -est
smell, -s, 10
smell, smelling, smelled, 10
smile, smiling, smiled, 5
smoke, 5
smoke, smoking, smoked, 5
snow
    much snow
snow, snowing, snowed
so
    so . . . that, 14
    not so . . . as, 15
soap, 4
some
somebody, 2, 12
someone, 2, 12
something, 1, 9, 12
    something is wrong, 12
    something is wrong with
        (something), 12
sometimes, 7
son, -s
song, -s
soon, -er, -est
sorry, sorrier, sorriest, 4
    to be sorry, 4

soul, -s, 7
sound, -s, 9
    to make a sound, 9
soup
sour, more —, sourest, 10
south
speak, speaking, spoke, spoken
special, more —, most —
spell, spelling, spelled
spend, spending, spent
spoil, spoiling, spoiled, 12
spoon, -s
sport, -s
spot, -s
spring, -s
stand, standing, stood, 2
start, starting, started
state, -s
    United States
statement, -s, 3
stay, staying, stayed
steal, stealing, stole, stolen, 7
step, -s, 5
step, stepping, stepped, 5
stick, sticking, stuck, 11
    to stick to (something), 11
sticky, stickier, stickiest, 11
still, -er, -est, 1
still, 5
stinginess, 3
stingy, stingier, stingiest, 3
stomach, -s, 10
stone, -s, 11
stop, stopping, stopped, 2
store, -s
story, stories

stove, -s
straight, -er, -est, 6
straighten, straightening,
    straightened, 6
strange, stranger, strangest, 5
strangely, more —, most —, 5
stranger, -s, 5
street, -s
strength, 7
strengthen, strengthening,
    strengthened, 7
strong, -er, -est, 7
structure, -s
student, -s
studies, 6
study, studying, studied, 6
stupid, more —, most —
subject, -s
substitute, -s, 2
sudden, more —, most —, 9
suddenly, more —, most —, 9
sugar
suit, -s
summer, -s
sun
Sunday
superlative
supper, -s, 3
surprise, -s, 6
surprise, surprising, surprised, 6
    to be surprised
sweep, sweeping, swept, 12
sweet, -er, -est, 10
swim, swimming, swam, swum
syllable, -s, 11
table, -s

tablecloth, -s, 12
take, taking, took, taken
    to take a bus
    to take care of (something), 5
    to take a long time, 10
    to take (something) off, 10
    to take place, 6
talk, talking, talked
tall, -er, -est
tame, tamer, tamest, 6
tar, 11
taste, -s, 10
taste, tasting, tasted, 10
tea
    a cup of tea
teach, teaching, taught
teacher, -s
tear, -s, 11
tear, tearing, tore, torn, 11
tell, telling, told
    to tell about (something), 6
    to tell a lie, 2
    to tell the truth, 2
temper, -s, 14
    to lose one's temper, 14
    to keep one's temper, 14
ten
tense
tenth
terrible, more —, most —, 13
test, -s
than
thank, thanking, thanked
    thank you
    thanks
that, 3, 6, 7

so . . . that, 14
the
theater, -s
their
theirs
then
them
themselves, 3
there
these
they
thief, thieves, 7
thin, thinner, thinnest, 7
thing, -s
think, thinking, thought
   to think about (something),
      7
third
thirsty, thirstier, thirstiest
thirteen
thirteenth
this
   this evening
   this time, 1
thorn, -s, 11
those
thousand, -s
   a thousand books
   thousands of people
thread, 12
thread, threading, threaded, 12
   to thread a needle
three
through
throw, throwing, threw, thrown

Thursday
ticket, -s
time, -s
   after a time, 3
   every time, 13
   from time to time
   to have time, 1
   once upon a time, 2
   to take a long time, 10
   this time, 1
   What time is it?
tired, more —, most —
   to be tired, 2
   to be tired of (something), 3
to
   to come up to (something), 8
   to the ends of the earth, 1
   from head to foot, 4
   to get to (somewhere), 15
   to point to (something), 1
today
together
tomorrow
   I'll see you tomorrow.
tongue, -s, 10
   a sharp tongue, 14
tonight
too, 2
   too dark to see, 7
tooth, teeth, 10
top, -s
toward, 4
town, -s
train, -s
   by train

travel, traveling, traveled
tree, -s
trip, -s
true
truth, 2
    to tell the truth, 2
try, trying, tried
    to try to (do something)
    to try (something) on
Tuesday
turn, turning, turned, 1
    to turn one's back, 1
    to turn around, 7
twelfth
twelve
twice
two

ugly, uglier, ugliest, 14
umbrella, -s, 4
unafraid, 2
uncle, -s
uncomfortable, more —, most —, 8
uncover, uncovering, uncovered, 15
under, 6
understand, understanding, understood
unfriendly, more —, most —
United States
until, 11, 13
up
    to come up to (something), 8
    to cover (something) up, 15

to get up, 2, 4, 15
to pick (something) up, 7
to put (something) up, 1
to sit up, 5
to wake up, 10
upon
    Once upon a time, 2
us
use, using, used
    used to, 14
usually, 7

vacation, -s
vegetable, -s
verb, -s
very
    Thank you very much.
    Very well, thank you.
visit, visiting, visited
vocabulary
voice, -s, 9

wagon, -s, 4
wait, waiting, waited
    to wait for (something), 4
    I can't wait to (do something), 13
wake, waking, waked, 10
    to wake up, 10
walk, walking, walked
    to walk along, 4
wall, -s
want, wanting, wanted
    to want to (do something)
warm, -er, -est, 10

was
wash, washing, washed
watch, watching, watched
water
  a glass of water
way, -s
we
weak, -er, -est, 7
weakness, -es, 13
wear, wearing, wore, worn
weather
Wednesday
weed, -s, 5
week, -s
weekend, -s
weigh, weighing, weighed, 6
weighmaster, -s, 8
weight, -s, 6
well, better, best
  Very well, thank you.
well, 13
well, -s, 11
were
west
what, 9
  What can we do about
    (something)? 11
  What can we do with
    (something)? 11
  What's your name?
  What time is it?
when, 1
where
which, 7
while, 15
whip, -s, 4

whip, whipping, whipped, 4
whipping, -s, 4
whiskey, 9
whistle, -s, 10
whistle, whistling, whistled, 10
white
who, 2, 7
whom, 7
whose
why
wide, wider, widest
wife, wives
wild, -er, -est, 6
will, 5
win, winning, won
window, -s
winter, -s
wise, wiser, wisest, 14
with
  something is wrong with
    (something), 12
  what can we do with
    (something)? 11
without, 3
woman, women
wonderful, more —, most —
wood, 10
  a piece of wood
  pieces of wood
woods, 2
word, -s
work
  to go to work
work, working, worked
  to work hard, 14
worry, worries, 6

worry, worrying, worried, 6
   to worry about (something),
     6
write, writing, wrote, written
writing, -s
wrong, 12
   something is wrong, 12
   something is wrong with
     (something), 12

yard, -s
year, -s
   a year ago

   next year
yell, yelling, yelled, 3
yellow
yes
yesterday
   yesterday afternoon
you
   It's good of you to come, 5
young
your
yours
yourself, yourselves, 3

# INDEX

175

Printer and Binder: Vail-Ballou Press Inc.

80 81 8 7 6 5 4